The research on which this report is based was commissioned and financed by the Gatsby Charitable Foundation to whom we are indebted.

Special thanks are due to all the long term unemployed people who overcame their concerns to take part in the focus groups and we are especially grateful to all those 'front line key workers' who gave us their time and trust and agreed to be interviewed despite sometimes having serious reservations about doing so.

We would also like to thank all the people in organisations that helped to facilitate the research and those who provided the focus group venues.

The report is also the first product of the close working relationship that has developed between the Unemployment Unit & Youthaid and the Welfare to Work Research Project at the University of Portsmouth.

Dan Finn directed the project and prepared the final report; Martin Blackmore carried out the fieldwork interviews and focus groups; and Matthew Nimmo reviewed the employment programme evaluation evidence.

Contents

SM. 980025'44

QFK J '11/99
8.99

Dan Finn, (Fin)
Martin Blackmore
and
Matthew Nimmo

Welfare-
to-work
and the
long term
unemployed

They're very cynical

Welfare-to-work and the long term unemployed: they're very cynical

Dan Finn, Martin Blackmore and Matthew Nimmo

Published by the Unemployment Unit & Youthaid

322 St John Street, London EC1V 4NT

The Unemployment Unit & Youthaid is a company limited by guarantee registered in England and Wales (no. 2458694).

©Unemployment Unit & Youthaid 1998

British Library Cataloguing in Publication Programme:

A catalogue record for this book is available from the British Library.

ISBN 1-870563-57-3

Printed by: RAP, 201 Spotland Road, Rochdale OL12 7AF

Designed by: BCreative, 12 Aldwych Place, Blackburn BB1 9QP

They're very cynical

ASW Actively Seeking Work

BA Benefits Agency

DfEE Department for Education and Employment

ES Employment Service

ESA Employment Service Adviser

ESJ Employment Service Jobcentre

FE Further Education

HB Housing Benefit

ILM Intermediate Labour Market. Local temporary work initiatives aimed at people out of work for over a years., which usually pay the 'rate for the job', are voluntary and carry out socially useful work.

JSA Jobseekers Allowance: replaced Unemployment Benefit and Income Support for unemployed people in October 1996. Payment is conditional on having drawn up and signed a Jobseeker's Agreement.

JSAg Jobseeker's Agreement: document detailing a claimant's availability for work and jobsearch strategy drawn up and signed by the claimant and their ESA at a New Jobseeker Interview.

JSD Jobseeker's Direction: power given to ESAs to direct a jobseeker to carry out certain activities that they consider will help them to find work.

SBR Stricter Benefits Regime: integral part of the Government's active labour market policy since 1986 aimed at strengthening the link between benefit payment and active jobsearch and keeping unemployed people in touch with the labour market. Measures include compulsory Restart interviews, compulsory remotivation programmes and benefit sanctions for inadequate jobseeking.

Employment Service programmes and initiatives

Caseload Interviews A series of structured interviews carried out on a one-to-one basis between an ESA and an unemployed person aimed at identifying the best way of getting work. In 1994 a 1-2-1 programme was introduced for young people aged between 18 and 25 who had been out of work for over a year. This was followed by a similar Jobfinder programme in 1996/97 aimed at those out of work for over two years.

Community Action
A temporary work programme, which operated between 1993 and 1996, aimed at those unemployed for over a year, who combined voluntary work with intensive job search activity for up to six month. Participants received benefit plus £10.

Community Programme
Large scale temporary work programme for the long term unemployed which operated between 1983 and 1988. Participants were paid the rate for the job and carried out work of community benefit for up to a year. An average wage funding formula meant that most participants worked part time and were young.

Employment Action
A short-lived small-scale temporary work programme which was replaced by Community Action.

Employment Training
The major training programme for unemployed adults which was introduced in 1988 and subsequently replaced by Training for Work.

Jobclub
Aimed at unemployed people who have usually been out of work for over six months. Participation can last for several months and involves guidance with job search skills, intensive job search activity and access to resources such as telephones, newspapers and stationery. Jobclub attendance is usually voluntary.

Jobfinders Grant
A national scheme introduced in 1995 which pays a grant of £200 to people who have been unemployed for two years over two years who find a full time job paying up to £150 a week.

Jobplan Workshop
A compulsory one week course, introduced in 1993, aimed at helping long-term unemployed people to set job goals and compete successfully for employment and training programme opportunities. Jobseekers were normally referred to Jobplan Workshop at their 12-month Restart interview.

North Norfolk Action
A small scheme for those unemployed for over six months which tested pilots in 'supportive caseloading' and temporary work in 1993/94.

Project Work
A pilot scheme introduced in 1996 aimed at 18 to 50 year olds unemployed for two years or more. It combined an initial period of up to 13 weeks intensive jobsearch assistance with an ESA followed by a 13 week

They're very cynical

mandatory work experience placement where participants received their benefit plus £10 a week.

Restart Courses

A compulsory two-week course, introduced in 1986, lasting two weeks combining half-day workshops with linked jobsearch activity. Jobseekers were normally referred to a Restart Course at their 24 month Restart interview.

Restart Interviews

A mandatory counselling interview which unemployed people are required to attend after each six months of unemployment. The aim is to review the job search activities of the unemployed person and an adviser will offer help from a 'menu' of programme opportunities to those who need extra assistance.

TfW

Training for Work. The main adult training programme, usually run by local Training and Enterprise Councils in England and Wales or Local Enterprise Companies in Scotland. TfW was available to those aged between 18 and 63 who have been unemployed for 6 months or more. In 1997/98 it has been replaced by Work Based Adult Training for the long term unemployed aged over 25.

TIS

The Travel to Interview Scheme. Assists Jobseekers to attend job interviews beyond the normal daily travelling distance of their home area by paying travel costs. To qualify for TIS a jobseeker must normally have been unemployed for 13 weeks.

Work Trials

Work Trials enable Jobseekers to work for potential employers on a trial basis for up to three weeks. During the period of the Work Trial Jobseekers continue to receive their JSA plus travel and meal expenses. A Jobseeker must normally have been unemployed for at least six months prior to the start of a Work Trial. If for any reason the Work Trial is unsuccessful, the Jobseeker continues to claim JSA and there are no benefit penalties.

Workstart

Pilot employment subsidy schemes aimed at the long term unemployed. The basic model was introduced in 1993 and offered employers six month subsidies of £60 a week for taking on people who had been unemployed for over two years. Other variations of payments and client groups were tried between 1995 and 1997.

Workwise

Intensive compulsory four week job serach assistance courses aimed at people aged between 18 and 25 who had been unemployed for over a year. Introduced nationally in 1995 and called 'Worklink' in Scotland.

T his report presents the findings of research carried out between June 1997 and March 1998. The aim of the project was to gather evidence on the views and experiences of long term unemployed people over the age of 25 and to provide a critical assessment of the programmes aimed at getting them back into work.

In the field research we carried out four case studies in areas of high unemployment where we both organised focus groups, attended by just under eighty long term unemployed people, and carried out lengthy interviews with over fifty 'street level' key workers in agencies delivering programmes for the unemployed. The desk research involved a comprehensive review of both published and unpublished evaluations of voluntary and compulsory programmes aimed at improving motivation and job search skills and at providing work experience.

The views of the unemployed

Overall we found that the attitudes of long term unemployed jobseekers in the four cities were remarkably consistent, despite very different employment biographies and local labour markets. The main findings from the focus groups were that:

● The vast majority of long term unemployed people in our sample expressed a strong desire to secure jobs and most said they were actively looking for work. However, they did not feel that the actively seeking work regulations or the Jobseekers Agreement had much relevance to their job search.

● Participants in our focus groups attributed unemployment to the lack of suitable job opportunities, but they also believed that employers hold negative stereotypes of those out of work for long periods. One major factor was ageism, though area based and racial discrimination were also involved.

● The jobseekers we spoke to wanted full-time permanent jobs that would pay them a 'living wage'. Part time and/or temporary work was an unattractive proposition, not because of the nature of the work - which some acknowledged could provide relevant work experience and a route into regular jobs - but because it meant disrupting a claim which threatened income security. This was particularly problematic for those receiving Housing Benefit and reinforces the case for tackling the rigidities of a benefit system that assumes a simple transition to full time permanent work.

- Many of those we talked with had sought out assistance with job search, but often found appropriate provision hard to access. Most of the younger participants accepted that they needed to acquire new skills. Unfortunately, access to good quality training or education was either expensive or difficult, or for some constrained by the limitations of the 16-hour rule. There was little enthusiasm for Government training schemes.

- Jobclubs were the most popular form of official assistance but there were criticisms that they were too inflexible in terms of access and attendance. Compulsory job search courses were resented and largely seen to be a waste of time, especially by those who were repeat attenders.

- Cynicism about 'government schemes' was widespread, and deeply felt. Most focus group participants were suspicious of the motives of the Employment Service and Government. While they wanted positive help in getting back to work, they believed that the primary aim of 'schemes' were to remove them from the unemployment register rather than provide them with genuine help.

- In general, the relationship between the claimants and the ES was poor. Claimant's think the ES handles the least attractive vacancies, is generally inefficient and too concerned with getting them into any available job. However, they appreciate that it is a difficult job for staff and some do establish good relationships with advisers. The problem of turnover amongst front line staff and advisers adds to the general impression of a non-caring, faceless bureaucracy. By contrast, the unemployed had a more constructive relationship with external agencies, especially those in the voluntary sector.

- The diversity of ES and other provision, and constant change, generates confusion amongst long term claimants regarding the names, nature and purpose of different schemes and programmes. Competition between providers helps add to the bewilderment among some members of the client group who were unable to distinguish between statutory and voluntary organisations and consequently between compulsory and voluntary participation. The overarching threat of benefit sanctions for inactivity (the message gets home) results in serial, acquiescent attendance at almost anything that is suggested to them (even our focus groups in some cases). The whole scenario does little to promote informed choice or reduce dependency.

- There was also much confusion about the detail of the benefit system and income tests. This acted as a major disincentive preventing unemployed people, for example, from taking advantage of casual job opportunities (which could help both improve their work skills and their income). It is crucial that this complexity is reduced and that the long-term unemployed are given clearer incentives to take up casual job opportunities, and to declare that fact to the DSS. More generally, complex benefit rules (and tax incentives) that are designed to increase incentives will not be effective unless potential recipients, and front line workers, know what the incentive is and understand how it works.

- Many of the long term unemployed people we interviewed felt threatened by and were hostile to what they saw as the new Government's 'cuts-driven' approach to welfare reform. The few who knew anything about the New Deal did not think it was of relevance to them.

The views of front line workers

The experienced front-line workers we interviewed were employed in a variety of statutory and voluntary agencies, and included a high proportion of current and former ES staff. The main findings were that:

- Most key workers attributed long term unemployment to a shortage of appropriate job opportunities and the tax/benefits poverty trap. However, they also stressed that some of the personal characteristics of the clients they worked with acted as barriers to employment. Some of these qualities were inherent to individuals, others, such as lack of recent work experience, were themselves the product of long periods of unemployment. Overall, there was broad agreement amongst ES staff, training providers and support workers that the fall in unemployment meant that those who were now long term unemployed need most support and will be the hardest people to find jobs for. The significant barriers that exist include physical and learning difficulties, problems with literacy and numeracy, mental health problems, substance abuse, poor communication and presentation skills, and insufficient access to adequate transport and other basic facilities like telephones.

- Most of the key workers acknowledged that the ES provided useful services but were generally critical of the impact of the stricter benefit regime. ES staff were themselves critical of high caseloads and the target culture which they worked within and suggested that the pressures these generated made it difficult for them to provide the individual support that was needed.

- There was much concern about the high turnover amongst ES workers, especially below adviser level, and also amongst the staff of external agencies. The high turnover amongst both groups had major implications for relationships between the ES and providers and for the effectiveness of policy implementation. For example, some front line ES staff lacked knowledge about the assistance available locally. Claimants had been directed to attend Jobclubs that no longer existed and TfW schemes that had been closed. Mis-information about the rules regarding part-time study and training on ESF courses caused confusion for claimants and unnecessary problems for providers. This could result in prospective trainees not availing themselves or having to abandon potentially useful opportunities. Particular problems were experienced in being able to take the time, and having the detailed knowledge and skills, to be able to give unemployed people accurate in-work benefits advice.

- Problems of turnover were exacerbated by inconsistency. For example, the degree of intensity with which ES staff scrutinised job search activity varied significantly, not only between different Jobcentres, but also within the same Jobcentre. In combination with the perceived irrelevance of much of the information sought this often left claimants unsure as to precisely what was expected of them.

● Providers of compulsory courses suggested that the main problem they experienced with mandatory participation was that it was often perceived as a threat or punishment, or as a way to inconvenience suspected fraudsters. Courses were sometimes disrupted, and often informally undermined, by those who resent being made to go which in turn prevents those who are genuinely seeking help from benefiting.

● The relationships between the various organisations involved in the 'unemployment industry' were complex. There were many examples of positive links between agencies, and especially between key staff working for providers and in the ES. However, there were problems that worked against the interests of claimants. For example, competition between various providers means that information is not always shared or communicated to clients. Competition for job placements is also strong and many external organisations work hard to develop exclusive relationships with prospective employers.

● Some of the problems with the referral to and delivery of ES programmes seemed due to contracted provider's inability to cope with fluctuations in demand. Many small organisations found it hard to compete for and deliver ES provision, and in all the areas covered key workers pointed to much 'turbulence' and instability amongst the provider network. Although larger provider organisations were better able to absorb these irregularities they too experienced much instability, arising from both policy changes as well as budget reductions. One of the most important 'knock-on' effects of the volatility of the market for delivering the full spectrum of employment and training programmes is that many front line staff are employed on short-term contracts, receive little training and frequently change jobs.

If one word epitomised the feelings of most of the long term unemployed people and key workers we talked to it was that of frustration. The feeling was expressed by claimants who were not able to find suitable work despite numerous job applications, and the acquisition of work experience and/or training. It was expressed by ES advisers who, because of high caseloads and performance targets, seemed unable to spend enough time with individual claimants to be able to offer the help they felt was needed. They were also frustrated because they often did not have the time they needed to find out about or monitor local projects in order to be able recommend them to claimants. In addition, even when they were aware of an initiative that looked as though it might be beneficial it might not be viable because of the restrictions imposed by unwieldy benefit regulations. Frustration was also expressed by those delivering contracted ES programmes who had to adhere to rigid specifications and what they thought to be outdated and often inappropriate programme manuals.

Findings from the evaluation studies

Many of the issues identified in the field research were also found in the evaluation studies. The research findings from **compulsory job search courses and caseloading interviews** showed that they have had mixed effects:

- While some have benefited from the assistance, others find it irrelevant at best, unnecessarily threatening at worst. In particular the evidence about Restart interviews and compulsory caseloading suggests that although this type of '1-2-1' support can get people into jobs quicker than otherwise it seems that the effect is reduced as provision is expanded. High quality Restart evidence also suggests that the effect may not last because of the short term and unstable nature of many entry-level jobs. It also seems that much of the reduction in unemployment associated with these programmes could have been achieved by people transferring to other benefits, or simply leaving the register, rather than being assisted into jobs. Nevertheless, the unemployed put a high value on being given clear, impartial and accurate information about jobs, training and other opportunities, and it is clear that genuine client-centered '1-2-1' advice, delivered by competent front line staff, could deliver the effective gateway they want.

- The provision of resources to unemployed people to aid their job search appears to be not only the most popular (with participants), but also the most cost effective, producing far higher job entry rates both before and after the effects of deadweight are considered. **Resource centres** such as those provided in Jobclubs should be expanded and, where not already provided, should be added to training and work experience programmes.

- ES staff have expressed concern about the unbalanced and increasing emphasis on job search programmes where "even popular and proven effective programmes like Jobclub seem 'tired' in the context of so much which focuses on improving jobseeking skills". They are also concerned about the confusion caused by having so many job search programmes with different names and eligibility requirements all offering much the same thing. A welcome response has been to begin to shift from the provision of large scale, rigidly structured job search programmes towards the modular approach now being developed through 'programme centres'. These can ensure more effective targeting by enabling claimants and advisers to customise and choose appropriate assistance.

- While job search assistance can help produce immediate results it is not clear that it has much effect on the long-term job prospects of participants. It may help individuals to enter work more quickly than otherwise, but it is predominantly their skill levels which will determine whether they return to unemployment, remain in low paid work, or progress up the employment ladder to greater security and earnings. A 'welfare to work' strategy will be better placed to tackle in-work poverty and dependency if the ES and other agencies can begin to develop employment retention, skill acquisition, and progression services.

They're very cynical

The **evidence from work experience programmes** is also mixed and the evaluation evidence is relatively weak because of the absence of control group studies. Nevertheless, the evaluations indicate that:

- Unemployed people and front line staff regard **voluntary temporary work programmes** delivering projects of community benefit with mixed feelings. Participants are fairly positive about the work they do and are pleased to have a chance to get back to work, even if only for a while. However, programmes paying a wage have typically offered part-time work which only young people with low housing costs and no family commitments could afford to take; yet benefit-plus payments are widely criticised for being inadequate or exploitative. Other criticisms have been about the quality of the work offered (manual work, or work in areas with poor job prospects) and lack of training; the short length of the placements; and the lack of connection with employers and with the regular labour market.

- The **compulsory Project Work programme** was regarded far less positively, particularly by those given little choice over their work placement.

- The evidence strongly suggests that so called **'Intermediate Labour Market' (ILM) programmes** which combine work experience paid at the rate for the job with formal training are significantly more effective than other programmes. They certainly have better gross job outcomes (though this may be partly accounted for by differences in recruitment). ILM programmes are somewhat more expensive but not by nearly as much as gross figures suggest. The problem with existing ILM programmes is that they offer fairly low wages and so exclude unemployed people in receipt of high levels of out of work benefit, such as older people with families and/or high housing costs. The answer could be to introduce a higher benefit-plus allowance, along the lines of the Community Work programme being piloted in Northern Ireland. Reforms to the tax and benefit system to 'make work pay' could also make waged temporary work programmes more attractive to the long term unemployed.

- The British evidence on **employment subsidies** gives few clues as to their likely impact on long term employment prospects. However, evidence from the recent Workstart pilots indicates that subsidised employees are likely to be kept on and that some net job creation takes place, especially amongst small firms (it was estimated that a new job opportunity was created in some 17% of the posts subsidised). However, getting work placements involved considerable administrative effort on the part of the ES and most of the jobs involved were unskilled and low paid. There will be formidable problems in getting enough employers involved to deliver the modest expansion in subsidies already announced for the two year plus unemployed, especially in competition with the subsidies on offer for the younger shorter term unemployed. If the very long term unemployed are to be made attractive to a larger group of employers it is likely that the subsidy will have to be the last stage in a sequence of support that has helped make the individual more 'job ready'.

- More positively, it seems that for some at least **work trials** can provide a much cheaper way of achieving some of the same effects as employment subsidies by allowing employers to try out a potential recruits for up to three weeks before appointing. So far, they have succeeded in helping the more employable out of work 'blue-collar workers' get jobs. They do have a strong potential role to play in a quality integrated job broking service, however, and if targeted at more disadvantaged unemployed people may help encourage employers to recruit people they would not otherwise have considered.

Key issues for programme success

Although the success of labour market programmes is very much dependent on the overall state of the labour market there is now a considerable body of evidence to show that the way in which programmes are implemented can be crucial in maximising their impact. In creating a new approach to long term unemployment, which more effectively tackles the legacy the new Government has inherited, it is vital that the new strategy:

- **Radically reforms the approach to performance and job entry targets.** The evaluation evidence showed two ways in which the target culture of the ES has undermined effectiveness. Firstly, rigid targets for the number of people being referred to programmes distorts ES priorities, prevents them from delivering a fully client-centred service, and means that too many people end up in programmes unsuitable for their needs. Secondly, inflexible job entry payment targets have encouraged bad practice and led to 'creaming', where participants are selected largely on the basis of how likely they are to get a job. While job entry rates are not irrelevant to programme effectiveness they mean very little on their own, and many programmes would add far more value if they helped those with the most severe labour market disadvantages. Although the development of more accurate measures of performance is a complex and demanding management task, it is crucial that in future providers and ES staff are allowed to have more input into developing those measures. If both groups are to improve the service they deliver, they need to have more confidence that the performance targets they work to are useful and relevant. In Reinventing Government' Osborne and Gaebler expressed the point bluntly: "saddling people with inappropriate measures in whose development they have had no input is a sure way to create resistance, destroy morale and encourage cheating" (1993, p.358).

- **Develops a client-centred advice and information service.** Unemployed people and ES staff express a clear need for the provision of impartial advice and information about jobs, training and other opportunities. Unfortunately, many existing ES opportunities have developed in a piecemeal fashion, lack coherence, and are too closely associated with the stricter benefit regime. It is also evident that too many ES staff know little about the array of employment and training opportunities and support available from external agencies including Further Education provision, Local Authority programmes, TEC or LEC local initiatives, voluntary sector ESF projects, and private sector services. The New Deal for 18 to 24 year olds has

They're very cynical

pointed reform in the right direction, with its emphasis on local partnerships, flexibility, individualised personal adviser support, and the development of local plans that included a mapping exercise of provision in their areas. It appears that this 'partnership' approach will be extended to the older long-term unemployed, but there will be formidable problems to overcome in translating the rhetoric of partnership into effective action. It is also not clear how these local partnerships will emerge, what their terms of reference will be, nor who they will be accountable too.

- **Introduces more flexible eligibility rules.** The existing system for rationing programme assistance, the detailed eligibility criteria, are far too complicated, can be contradictory, and are not easily understood by claimants or staff. Most programmes currently have exemptions to allow early entry to special groups, such as people with disabilities or ex-offenders, but the list seems arbitrary and unfair especially for those who move in and out of low paid short-term and seasonal jobs. Many of the individuals concerned are already disadvantaged in labour market terms yet if they take up these job opportunities they find it even harder to meet relevant eligibility conditions. In part, this could be remedied by using criteria based on the number of months spent in unemployment in the previous two years. Also, while duration related eligibility rules are a useful tool for ensuring that programmes are more cost-effective it may be time for the ES to develop more sophisticated screening tools which could enable it to identify and assist those at high risk of long term unemployment at an earlier stage. Early assistance could be both more effective, in building on recent work experience, and cheaper.

- In the longer term it should be possible to build on the experience of the Government's new Employment Zones to create an **individual entitlement approach based on personal job accounts.** If funds could be more generally allocated to areas instead of being channelled through discrete programmes, each with their own categorical and sometimes conflicting objectives and eligibility rules, greater flexibility could be created. It could then be possible that after assessing individual barriers to employment personal advisers could access a pool of funds, allocated according to the barriers faced, with which they could purchase appropriate assistance.

Rights and responsibilities: benefit sanctions and programme attendance

Unemployed people and front line staff have mixed attitudes about compulsion. Many agree with the principle and accept it as a safeguard against abuse, yet suggest in practice it is applied inappropriately and sometimes unfairly. What unemployed people most resent is compulsion without a genuine range of choice. Project Work was objected to most vehemently by those who were given little or no choice of work experience placement. It is not the compulsory nature of Restart interviews which is resented so much as the fact that unemployed people (and ES staff) feel that clients' own needs and long-term goals are ignored in favour of targets aimed at achieving short-term outcomes. There is also evidence that interventions are less effective than they could be because providers have to deal with reluctant participants who can be hard to control and disruptive to those participants who want to be there.

While positive interventions can assist the long term unemployed return to work there is a significant danger that if the programmes involved are perceived as compulsory this will also alienate rather than attract employers. The evidence shows that the main concern of employers is that the long term unemployed will not have the 'right' work attitudes and motivation, and that this is more of a barrier than low levels of (or outdated) skills. As Atkinson and colleagues have pointed out "unemployed people taking part in a voluntary programme are already half way to proving their commitment to possible employers, (and) it is unlikely that graduates of a compulsory scheme, recruited under threat of benefit sanctions, will be seen .. as embodying the necessary positive attitudes to the world of work" (ESC, 1997, p. 101).

The new Government has kept in place much of the legal framework of compulsion that it inherited. Indeed it has made sanctions slightly tougher for those able bodied unemployed young people who refuse to participate in the New Deal. However, it does seem to be trying to create a different overall approach. For young people New Deal compulsion should be the last stage of a process involving individual guidance and real choice between a range of options. For the older unemployed, the aim appears to be that the requirement to attend courses should be applied more flexibly, especially in those areas that are developing programme centres. At the same time, the formal targets of the ES have been amended to focus on labour market assistance rather than benefit policing measures. Unfortunately, as we embark on a period of great potential the danger is that the public rhetoric of 'rights and responsibilities', with its apparent emphasis on compulsion, could be sending the wrong signal both to the unemployed, to front line staff, and to employers.

W ithin Government and the policy making community it is now widely sug gested that many of the long-term unemployed need active assistance if they are going to be able to access the jobs being generated by economic growth. It has also been suggested that radical reform of the benefit sys tem is needed to both enhance work incentives and stimulate more active and effective job search.

The previous Conservative Government adopted an approach that combined labour market de-regulation with a stricter benefit regime, culminating in the introduction of the Jobseekers Allowance in 1996. The cumulative effect of its policies was to reduce the real value of out of work welfare payments; to reinforce work incentives, particularly through in-work benefits; and to promote more job search through increased activity testing and scrutiny. This was underpinned by compulsory participation in a variety of job search, training and remotivation courses for those out of work for over a year. Despite some progress in modernising the system, and the successful reduction in unemployment generated by economic recovery, the number of those out of work for over a year remains high. By March 1998, according to the Labour Force Survey, this total stood at 486,000 - of which two thirds have been unemployed for more than 2 years. At the same time the Employment Service, and government 'schemes', have become unpopular, and many of the long-term unemployed are sceptical about their value and their aims.

The Labour Government, elected in 1997, has made it clear that tackling this legacy and implementing radical welfare reform is one of its major objectives. Although the new benefit regime created through the 1996 Jobseekers Act will be maintained, the new Government has suggested that increased claimant responsibilities will be balanced by access to new high quality employment and training programmes. However, despite the laudable aims of Government Ministers, there are fundamental problems ahead. As one front line ES adviser put it to us:

> *The problem we're going to have is actually convincing the clients that this is all new, and will actually make a difference. Many of them have already been through the whole battery of schemes and, you know, they're very cynical.*

Many of the long term unemployed people we interviewed were hostile to what they saw as a cuts-driven approach to welfare reform, and of those that knew anything about the New Deal few thought that it was of any relevance to them.

This is hardly surprising. So far most attention and resources have been focussed on the Government's New Deal for the younger unemployed. For this group, extensive consultation has taken place, focus groups have been held with young people throughout the country (some of which have been attended by Ministers), and over £2½ billion of the revenues raised by the windfall tax have been allocated to creating new opportunities for them.

By contrast little attention has been given to exploring the experiences of the older long term unemployed, a group who have been allocated far fewer resources under the New Deal. As the Government begins to develop its programmes for the older unemployed, it seemed vital that their views and experiences should receive the same attention that has been given to their younger counterparts. We also wanted to investigate the views and experiences of the front line key workers who deliver Government programmes. Both groups, who do not figure highly in the policy making process, have accumulated a wealth of knowledge and insights into the workings of the system.

In addition to collecting this information another aim of the research was to gain some insights into how both groups actively negotiate and actually make sense of the plethora of initiatives, programmes and benefit regulations which together aim to tackle welfare dependency.

The aim of this critical assessment of the experiences of the long-term unemployed and of the legacy of Conservative policy is to help highlight the weaknesses in previous programmes in order to better guide future policy developments.

The report

This report presents the findings of research carried out between June 1997 and March 1998. The main aim of the research was to provide an independent evaluation of UK unemployment policies for the long term unemployed drawing heavily on the perspectives of those who are affected by them and those who implement them on a day-to-day basis. Our primary objective was not to find particular fault, but rather to see what lessons could be learned from an open, candid and in-depth appraisal of present circumstances.

The first section reports the findings of the field research that was carried out between September and December 1997. Overall we carried out four case studies in areas of high unemployment where we both organised focus groups, attended by just under eighty long term unemployed people, and carried out lengthy interviews with over fifty 'street level' key workers (see Appendix A for more details about the research aims, methodology, and the composition of those interviewed).

The second section contains the findings of desk research where we reviewed much of the UK evidence about the effectiveness of programmes aimed at tackling long term unemployment, especially those programmes delivered through the ES. This section draws on both published and

They're very cynical

unpublished evaluations and we were particularly concerned to draw out what evidence existed on the experiences and perceptions of the unemployed users.

Labour market programmes and the New Deal

Previous British Governments have now experimented with a vast array of interventions, ranging from direct assistance with job search, and the costs of taking up work, through to work experience programmes, employment subsidies, help with starting small businesses and training and education schemes. The evaluation literature is also vast, although much of the evidence about actual programme effects consists of sample survey results or follow-ups of participants. There have actually been few examples of more technically sophisticated attempts to establish 'net' effects and impacts by using control groups. For these reasons we do not, in the second section, attempt to use the very different types of evaluation data to compare programmes with one another in terms of cost-effectiveness. Such comparisons may appear to give a simple guide to policy-making but, by not comparing like with like, can produce misleading results.

We also decided, for reasons of time and space, to concentrate on evaluations of particular types of programmes - job search assistance; Restart and 'caseloading' interviews; work experience and intermediate labour market programmes; employment subsidies; and work trials. In part this reflects the trends put in place by the last Government which, in the 1990s, dramatically shifted the focus of its active labour market measures away from longer duration training schemes towards shorter mandatory job search courses. Although in 1997/98 most expenditure was still allocated to training, the number of participants involved in job search courses was vastly greater. In contrast with the 212,000 people who were expected to participate in Training for Work, it was anticipated that over 850,000 long term unemployed people would participate in either job search assistance programmes or be placed on ES adviser caseloads for an intense sequence of interviews.

The choice of the evaluations we assessed also reflected the likely direction of Labour policy. The Government has now moved beyond its initial priority of establishing the New Deal for 18 to 24 year olds, and changes are now beginning to take place in its approach towards the older long-term unemployed. A New Deal for those out of work for over two years is to be launched in June 1998, and follows the creation in February of five pilot Employment Zones for those out of work for over a year. New Deal pilot schemes, covering 90,000 of those out of work for a year or 18 months, are to be launched in November 1998. At the same time ES programmes for the rest of the older unemployed are being reorganised.

As the Government develops its new approach, and as local partnerships begin to tackle the problems faced by the long-term unemployed, it is vital to understand the perspectives of the unemployed and of those working most closely with them. Otherwise, despite much local energy and enthusiasm, there are dangers that instead of tackling the mistakes of the past they could be compounded.

Part one

FOCUS GROUP AND INTERVIEW FINDINGS

1. Looking for work

Of the 78 people who took part in the focus group discussions all but one expressed a desire to find full-time paid employment and claimed that they were actively seeking work. The degree of job search activity varied considerably. Even though some individuals were pessimistic about their chances and had been unemployed for a number of years most were making intensive and repeated efforts to secure employment. Others, who admitted to being less active, felt that the likelihood of them finding a job was very slim regardless of duration of unemployment. Victims of redundancy tended to be more pessimistic and this was noticeable among older people who had previously held skilled jobs and managerial positions. A small group of participants were not making strenuous efforts to find work at the time because they were engaged in activities aimed at improving their employability such as training and education courses.

When probed about their actual job search activities most focus group participants cited their local newspaper/s as the best place to look for work. Very few of them had approached, or registered with, private employment agencies and most were sceptical about making speculative enquiries to employers which they tended to see as something they were increasingly expected to do by the ES. There was a general consensus amongst focus group participants that the Jobcentre had the least attractive jobs.

Jobcentres

Amongst the focus group participants there was a pervasive consensus that their local Jobcentres were not very efficient at advertising vacancies and attracted the least attractive jobs locally. Some people repeated well-known criticisms about the inefficiency of the system with regard to updating vacancy notices:

> *When you go for jobs in the Jobcentre.... and you go up to the girl or woman and both jobs are gone...that's happened to me a few times. Why don't they take the card down if it's gone? You've waited in the queue for two jobs, that's all you're allowed anyway in the Jobcentre, and you go up and the jobs are gone and you've wasted half an hour in the queue before they've even called your name out.*

They're very cynical

*When you sign your contract [the Job Seeker's Agreement] now, you're con-
tracted to go there [the Jobcentre] three times a week anyway so every time you
go in there, there's the same jobs.*

*It's crap, isn't it? If the job hasn't gone, you must be 15,000 behind the rest of
them [others seeking work]. It's the last place to look [for work]. And if you start
looking at them [Jobcentre notice-boards], you realise how little they change.
The 'News' is better actually and also looking in some Employment Agencies,
though I haven't got anything out of them.*

Some people disliked the direct spatial link between looking for work and claiming benefits:

*I dislike the atmosphere in there [the Jobcentre] because you're like the under-
dog. You're made to feel not like a job-seeker but like a sponger.*

*The only reason people go to the Jobcentre is to get their giro. They [Jobcentres]
take away all your dignity, don't they? If you didn't have to sign on to get your
giro, the Jobcentres would be empty. They wouldn't need their security guard!
It's [the Jobcentre] a good front though, init? People see the Jobcentre and they
say "oh, at least there's a Jobcentre there, there must be some jobs around."
They'd be better off to give you a phone-card that was only allowed to be used
for [calling] employers and a free copy of the News and they'd get more people
off the dole like that.*

Many participants were critical of the actual jobs advertised in Jobcentres. Some people felt that
a number of the vacancies were submitted by what they considered to be unscrupulous employers:

*To be honest, I think that the people who are advertising in the Jobcentre, the
employers, are dodgy bastards anyway. They're the ones that wouldn't dare put
in the paper what they want to pay you.*

*Also you do get companies, cowboy companies, who are offering funny jobs
where you are going to get ripped off if you take the job, self-employed types,
commission-only...so a lot of the work, it won't set a salary, it'll say negotiable.*

Employers use the Jobcentre as the last resort. They've tried every other avenue to get people in,
the unemployed is the last chance. Also it gives them [employers] an air of legitimacy when they
use government channels to employ people...nobody's going to check up on the employers.

By far the most prevalent view however was that the bulk of the vacancies advertised in Jobcentres
offered unacceptably low wages:

Welfare-to-work and the long term unemployed

There are some good jobs displayed in there but the point is that they're for skilled people and the odd one or so that's for non-skilled has a wage of about £2.50 an hour.

£3.50 an hour is OK for someone, a youngster, living at home with mum and dad but it's not on for someone like us [older with family responsibilities] and the majority of jobs down in the Jobcentre are in that wage bracket. Very rarely will you see a job at over £5 an hour unless you're a skilled plumber or something. If a job comes up at over £4 an hour, you'll get over a hundred people going for it, for one job!

In some ways, there are more jobs than ever in Britain now but when you go to the Job Centre and look at ones on offer you can't take them because of the low wages or the age requirements.

If you went into the Jobcentre and removed those jobs that were below £200 a week, you'd probably have only about three cards left on the board and they'd be slightly iffy jobs, you know like commission-based pay.

A Jobcentre worker had some sympathy with these views. She said that most employers who used Jobcentres were the ones that didn't want to spend money on advertising and were paying 'rock bottom wages'. Two Jobcentre workers from different offices claimed that they had often tried to persuade such employers to offer higher wages and complained that the ES had no powers to refuse to advertise what they considered to be poorly paid jobs.

Opinions varied among those who work with the long-term unemployed as to what were the most appropriate job search strategies. A former Jobclub leader argued that the more jobs a person applied for the higher the chances were that they would eventually find work. Support workers in voluntary employment access centres however suggested that it was demotivating for clients if they made repeated job applications only to get repeated rejections. This only served to reinforce pessimistic attitudes and, even if successful, was likely to result in the client being unemployed again quite quickly because they had taken a job that was not suitable. A more focused and selective approach to job seeking was favoured by most key workers including some of those in official Jobclubs. Such a strategy was considered to be out of kilter with ES policy but in the client's long-term interests. A training provider made some similar observations:

Some people need to do the 100 applications. However, I reckon if it's somebody reasonably able, reasonably skilled and reasonably literate I can get them a job with three applications. You target the right job and you make sure they've got the skills for it. If someone's gone through a training course then you know what skills they've got and you target the jobs that need those skills. There is no point in making people apply for a quota simply for the sake of it. What they've got to be is assisted to apply for appropriate, relevant jobs.

Jobsearch and the active benefit system

Over the past ten years unemployed people have been increasingly required to show that they are actively seeking work and, since 1996, have been required to enter into a written contract with the ES called the Jobseeker's Agreement (JSAg). This 'agreement' sets out the details of the claimant's proposed weekly job search strategy and no benefit is paid until such an agreement is agreed, drawn up and signed. In 1996 ES Advisers were also given the legal power to issue a Jobseeker's Direction (JSD) requiring a claimant to take specified steps to improve their employment prospects or face a benefit sanction.

We wanted to get the views of those affected by the changes in order to get some sense of the overall impact on the job seeking behaviour of the long term unemployed. We wanted to find out what claimants felt about these new rules generally and also about their experiences of complying with them. Similarly, we also wanted to discover how ES staff were using their new powers and implementing the job seeking requirements.

Most focus group participants felt that the requirement to look for work as a condition of benefit entitlement was acceptable in principle. The following quote typifies the initial response to questions about the actively seeking work rules:

> I think that if you're unemployed, the least that you can do is look for work during the week and turn up for your interview with the written proof that you have looked for work rather than turn up at the Job Centre with an empty sheet. It's fair.

However, most focus group participants qualified such remarks with misgivings about the manner and context in which the obligation to look for work was implemented. Some had reservations about the practicalities of proving that you were actually trying to look for work:

> The principle is OK but it's the way that it's being enforced. Sometimes you try for jobs but you don't even get a reply from the employer and so you can't really prove that you have made an application.

> It is totally unreasonable to want people to actively seek work when there's no work there. The other thing is how do you prove it? How can you be sure that people are really looking for work and applying for so many jobs a week? That's the thing.

One man felt that the rules were acceptable provided they were applied to everyone equally. He suspected however that the rules were not applied uniformly and that some claimants who were not genuinely seeking work were being left alone because they were too troublesome:

> They always check mine [Activity Log] but I feel that they're checking the people who are doing things and not checking those that can't be bothered because it's easier for them just to check the ones that are doing the stuff.

Some older people highlighted the distinction between a passive and an active benefit system. They felt that the move towards an active system was inappropriate for them personally because they felt they were entitled to benefits by virtue of National Insurance contributions:

> *It's not morally right is it because you could have paid in all your life, coming up to retirement, you know what I mean, never took anything from the government and suddenly you've got to go to all these interviews and no-one wants to employ you, fifty-seven years of age for instance, you've got no chance whatsoever of getting another job but you've still got to go to the interviews.*

A training provider expressed similar reservations about requiring older long-term unemployed to show that they were actively seek work:

> *There needs to be a cut-off point, I mean there are men of 59 being hassled to find work… They're probably never going to work so why hassle them? Forget them, pension them off or whatever*

An ES staff member identified categories of claimant for whom she felt the new rules were inappropriate:

> *If you look at the unemployed two year plus you've got quite a few big categories in there. You've got the ones that are say like over fifty, right, who have perhaps worked all their lives and they see this as like "well I've paid in to the system so I'm getting the benefits" and they are just literally cruising to retirement. You've got those. You've got the care in the community ones who are absolutely loco, and you, well, you just wouldn't ask them even what their name is you know, and they just literally come in and sign. You've got the ones maybe who genuinely want to work, but for some reason they've got either literacy or numeracy problems, or sort of behavioural problems, that make it difficult.*

Most ES staff thought that the principle was reasonable, that the requirement could act as a useful 'prod', but they were deeply concerned about the impact that random speculative approaches could have on employer perceptions and goodwill:

> *It might make a difference to a few, they might just get lucky. It might have been something that that person needed to actually get them going again. I mean we do get people who are two years plus [unemployed] getting jobs.*

> *In the end it's bound to have a detrimental effect on us losing the custom of the employers because if you're just sending people that aren't really suited to the job, or you know they're not going to turn up but you have to refer them anyway, it's just wasting everyone's time really, and it's bound to have a knock-on effect. You see it now, on the actual system employers are saying, you know, "can you please make sure that client [jobseeker] turns up for interview as client [employer] has had lots of did not attends."*

Evidence of jobsearch

The formalities of providing evidence of job search are not clear-cut. When an unemployed person first makes a claim for JSA they are advised at an interview to keep a record of what they do each week to find work. To this end many are issued with an 'activity log' which they can use to record their job search activities. Technically however they are not legally obliged to keep a written record, but they must be able to demonstrate that they have been actively seeking work when they attend their fortnightly reviews. At the fortnightly reviews ES staff are supposed to run a check on what claimants have been doing to find work in the previous two weeks and also refer them to any suitable vacancies. If there is any doubt about a claimant's commitment to find work then ES frontline staff are supposed to refer the claimant to an ES Adviser .

We were interested in finding out how these new rules worked in practice. For example, whether claimants had experienced difficulties in providing evidence of job search activity and whether ES staff had experienced any problems checking the veracity of job search declarations.

It soon became apparent that there was a wide variation in the experiences of individual focus group participants. Put simply, there was no apparent consistency in the application of the actively seeking work regulations in any of the four areas. Different claimants encountered different ap-proaches in the same office whilst some claimants encountered different approaches when they had transferred from one office to another. The focus group participants who attended one of two Jobcentres in the same area recounted the following experiences:

> It [checking the activity-log] depends on where you sign on. You can get away with murder in [Jobcentre # 1], you could be unemployed for fifty years and they wouldn't do anything! I noticed a real difference when I moved house and started signing on at [Jobcentre # 2] and when I got in there, it was suddenly on the screen and it was, like, "Well, what have you done [to find work]? .. It de-pends who is behind the desk. There are people who always insist on seeing them [activity logs] and people who just say "Ah well, carry on."

> If they're having a good day, you're going to get a good day, do you know what I mean. If they're having a shit day they're going to give you so much crap. I don't think it's "Oh, we like him, we'll sort him out", it's just human nature, do you know what I mean. There was one person and I always wanted to sign on with her because she wasn't going to give you a lot of grief, like. She wasn't one of the more vicious ones who really did take a dislike to you.

Some focus group participants claimed that there was little application of the rules:

> They don't really have time to check whether you're doing everything they tell you to do as there's always a big queue so you just go in sign on and then you go out. They don't have time to ask about anything.

Welfare-to-work and the long term unemployed

They don't hound you about the proof though. They check your Activity Log now and then but some of them can't be bothered because it's more work for them.

Conversely, some other focus group participants were checked up on and had become very cautious since the introduction of the new regulations:

Sometimes they think you're lying, init? You go up there and you sign on and they, like, lob all the truth out of you and they take it and cross-check you on it, like "Are you sure it was this day?" do you know what I mean?

Ten or fifteen years ago it probably wasn't as bad then but, like, because of all the changes and all the suspicion and trying to get people off the dole, that's why all these things have been brought in, init? All these things have made people more suspicious.

Any little thing now and they [Jobcentre staff] can tick you off and cut your money.

For some focus group participants the new regulations had had little impact on their labour market position; rather they had created a perverse incentive to lie in order to safeguard their benefits:

When you go there [the Jobcentre], right, to sign on you gotta lie. They [Jobcentre staff] tell you that you gotta do this, you gotta do that, so you go down there and lie, do you know what I mean? There's a lot more questions than there used to be as to why you're unemployed.

As far as I am concerned it is a load of rubbish in as much as while you're answering the questions you are so fearful of being taken off benefits that you aren't truthful.

None of the focus group participants in our sample had experienced any serious difficulties with the new regulations, either with regard to providing evidence of job search activity or being challenged about the veracity of their evidence. However a Jobclub leader in one area said that she had two clients who had been sanctioned for not providing written evidence of their job search. One was a Vietnamese man who's written English "wasn't wonderful"; the other was an Asian man who had his benefits suspended for "not keeping accurate records of his job search".

Policing jobsearch requirements

When we asked ES staff about their experiences of implementing JSA all of them said that it had not been fully implemented. Most of them explained that there was insufficient staff time in their particular office in order to conduct all the necessary procedures:

They're very cynical

I don't know if JSA has been implemented by the letter of the law anywhere. It certainly hasn't been here.

All you get in reality now is people desperately trying to clear queues, just get 'em out. They call it 'fast-signing'. What you're supposed to do is, a person comes in, you're supposed to say 'how's the job search been going, what types of things are you looking for, let's do a job search with you, try and get you on something'. For everyone, every fortnight...it's actually classed as an interview now, not 'signing on'. But what really happens is 'volumetrics' where you divide the number of claims by the number of staff, and that gives you the time you can spend with each client. We get seven minutes for each client because we're so short staffed so we just say 'sign here'.

As it stands it's unworkable, people just don't do it, they can't be bothered with all that nonsense. You'd need about ten times the staff and ten times the time.

One ES staff member argued that even if the staff resources were made available JSA would still be unworkable:

Even if you had the staff to implement JSA properly you still couldn't match the people we see to the jobs we've got on offer, it's just not as simple as that.

The actively seeking work regulations are a part of what is known as the Stricter Benefit Regime (SBR). The SBR was developed in the late 1980s and encompasses a range of measures aimed at tightening the eligibility criteria for receiving benefits coupled with the increasing use of benefit sanctions for contravention of the regulations. In 1994 the SBR was stepped up when ES staff were given a new target for submitting claims to Adjudication Officers where there was doubt about a claimant's availability or willingness to work. None of the ES staff we spoke to said that they were keen to impose sanctions on claimants and most said that they were reluctant to do so. However some reported that they knew of other members of staff who were, in their opinion, over zealous when it came to referring suspected claimants to Adjudication:

Some Advisers in (another local Jobcentre) love SBR because if at the end of the day you can't do anything with a client, you've always got SBR to fall back on. So with APA targets you know that if you were to suspend that person for two weeks you'll get a result.

Such people were thought to be the exception rather than the rule. During the course of the interviews a number of ES staff said that since the change of government there had been an unofficial consensus that the SBR was to be pursued less vigorously. One frontline worker put it this way:

At the moment the message seems to be coming down from above - 'cool it on SBR', try and submit them to jobs, try and get them on training or FE or whatever but leave SBR as the last option.

The Jobseeker's Agreement and Jobseeker's Direction

When JSA was introduced in 1996 the SBR was strengthened with the introduction of the Jobseeker's Agreement (JSAg) and the Jobseeker's Direction (JSD). The JSAg replaced the old Back to Work Plan which was an advisory and voluntary document that outlined the steps a claimant would take each week to find work. The JSAg is a much more elaborate document that not only details explicitly the claimant's job seeking steps, but is also a binding agreement with attached benefit penalties for non-compliance. We wanted to find out how claimants felt about entering into such a contract and whether they had experienced any difficulties in negotiating and drawing-up the agreement.

None of the focus group participants felt that the JSAg was either useful or worthwhile and most of them were quite disparaging about it:

> When I did mine, I said that I went to certain agencies and what not and if I didn't really want to work I could have said all of that and it wouldn't have made any difference. Just because I as an individual do want a job, but once you know what the game is you just say anything to get your Giro at the end of the week. That's your main concern.

> It's a joke, a waste of paper. You sit there with a person who knows nothing about you and they're obviously in a rush so you get about ten minutes of their time and then you sign it and then go.

> When people go into the Jobcentre to do those forms, they're not really fo-cused on what they're going to be doing to find employment, they're more focused on what do I have to do to make sure that I get my bloody Giro? That's the real issue, you know.

There were a number of complaints from focus group participants about the way in which the JSAg was drawn up. Most of these complaints concerned a lack of negotiation between the claimant and the ES Claimant Adviser. A number of focus group participants also felt that they had been "conned" into signing their JSAg:

> We had a discussion and he said, "Well, you're doing everything that you can to find work". He then printed off a print-off, went over to another machine to get it, gave it to me, facedown, and said, "Sign here to show that you've been and you've done it". So I signed this form and when I got home I turned it over and on the back it said, "You will visit the Job Club, you will phone an employer, you will do this..." Now, I never agreed to any of that. So the next time I went in to sign on I handed it back to them and I said, "I'm not accepting this is, I never agreed to this, I want to see someone about it, why was this put in without my knowledge?" And they said, "Oh, that's all right" and slipped it into my file and

it's still on file! I'm not saying that I wouldn't do it, I'm just saying that I never made that agreement so therefore I don't feel bound by it.

They just get you to sign it and put it in their computer and you can't see the screen. Then they give it to you and you sign it. He didn't open the thing up and say, "Look, this is what we agree to, will you sign this?" In the discussion that I had, I never agreed to any of this going to the Jobcentre every week or phoning an employer every week, or writing so many letters every week, that never ever entered into the discussion.

Basically I thought that I was just having a chat with him but all he was doing was programming everything I said to him into the computer and I just realised it afterwards. He gave me this to sign [shows copy of the JSAg] but I didn't know what I had signed until afterwards because he had folded it over like that [demonstrates with copy of JSAg]. He just gave me like a massive package. I realised as I walked away, what's going to happen is that one of these days I'm going to go in there [the Jobcentre] and they're going to say "What have you been doing? These are your commitments. You signed them".

What they just do is that they've got a standard form and they know what they expect to be on it and they rattle it off to you and there's no way you're going to say "Stop! I can't do that or I can't do that". There is no negotiation because then your money stops, you see. It's dictated to you.

The second element of the SBR introduced as part of the JSA regulations was the Jobseeker's Direction (JSD). The JSD is a power given to ES Advisers enabling them to direct jobseekers to improve their employability through things like attendance on courses aimed at improving job seeking skills or motivation.

None of the focus group participants had been subject to a JSD but ES staff said that JSDs had been used to refer some claimants to things like training courses and Jobclubs. A number of providers confirmed that they had had claimants referred to them via JSDs. One Jobclub leader however felt that the JSD was being used inappropriately in her area:

They direct them here for a fortnight which can make life difficult because we want people in Jobclubs that are voluntary, not just sent here for a fortnight for the hell of it. They're using it instead of Restart in some respects. We could probably turn it around if we had them for longer than a fortnight but it's not really long enough to do anything useful.

This was not an isolated case; a Jobclub leader in another area made an almost identical comment. One ES staff member said that there was a reluctance to use the JSD in her office because

Welfare-to-work and the long term unemployed

of the added administrative workload. However she claimed that ES Advisers sometimes directed claimants to do certain things without using the official backing of a formal written JSD:

> The Advisers don't really tend to use them that often. They've got the power to do it but they're very reluctant because again, it is more work than it's worth. You tend to get general ones like "get a CV produced" or "go down to a Jobclub to have a look and see what it's like." They aren't the sort of harsh ones; they tend to be used for the people that sort of need a bit of a kick... You tend to find it's easier for an Adviser to see somebody and say "I want you to do this and I'll see you in a fortnight's time" rather than go through all the rigmarole of doing a Direction on the system, and they tend to do it that way.

Private employment agencies

In all four locations, training providers and support workers reported a noticeable growth in the numbers of private employment agencies, particularly over the past two years. Our research indicates however that this growth in the number of agencies is unlikely to have a major impact on long-term unemployment due to prejudices on both sides. The claimants we spoke to did not see private employment agencies as providing a service. Rather they thought that the relationship was exploitative. At its most extreme agencies "might pay £2.50 an hour while they're screwing £7 or £8 an hour.... just sat on their arse, parasites, aren't they?" Alternatively, agencies are "a bunch of fly bastards making money out of people's misery". For "every week's wage that you get when you're working for an agency, that agency takes 10% of your wages". More commonly "the agencies offer temporary jobs and they're not interested in giving you long-term work."

It could be that these perceptions act as a self-imposed barrier to employment. However, according to many of the training providers and support workers we spoke to, the perceptions that agency staffs' have about the long-term unemployed also act as a barrier. Training providers and support workers who used agencies as potential sources of vacancies for their clients suggested that agencies generally were only interested in those whom they considered 'work-ready':

> The agencies, by and large, don't really want people who've been unemployed for more than six months... They make assumptions about their work readiness. And on one level you can say, well alright, an agency actually needs somebody to be absolutely work ready because there's no leeway here, you know, they've got to go on site, they've got to do the job straight away.

There were a few exceptions to this general rule where individual support workers had developed close working links with particular agencies. The success of the relationship relied heavily on trust between individual agency staff and key workers as well as the support workers' ability to work closely with their clients

Weasked all of those we had contact with what they thought were the main
barriers preventing the long-term unemployed from finding work. In gen
eral, although not exclusively, claimants tended to focus on what they con
sidered to be externally imposed barriers such as employers' attitudes and
prejudices, the labour market, wage levels and the benefits system. The
responses from key workers were more varied. The majority echoed much of what the claimants
had said regarding external barriers, although some considered aspects such as wage levels and
the benefits trap to be self-imposed restrictions reflecting the perceptions, aspirations and attitudes of claimants. An additional element in many key workers' responses were factors related to
the personal characteristics and qualities of individual clients. Some characteristics, such as inse-
curity and motivation, were often said to be symptomatic of long periods of unemployment,
whilst personal qualities such as level of social skills and aptitude were often regarded as longer
term individual characteristics.

Discrimination

Ageism was identified as an externally imposed barrier to employment and was consistently referred to, although emphasised to different degrees, by claimants and key workers alike. Focus
group participants in all four areas cited numerous examples of ageist attitudes on the part of
employers:

> I went for a general stores job, it was to keep the place tidy, to do a bit of
> paperwork. The chap looked up and said, "What age are you?" I said, "I'm 42, I
> could do this job." And I could have done the job standing on my head but he
> said "But you're over 35." I said, "Are you telling me honestly that I'm too old to
> sweep the floors?" and he said "Yeah, we are looking for somebody under 35."

> Age is a big part of it for me. They don't say outright that it's the age that puts
> them off but you are often asked your age... and you just get a feeling about it.
> Also, so many job advertisements specify age, you know, up to 35, even those
> for mature people are for people up to the age of 40 or something like that.

A training provider whose courses are designed for the older unemployed claimed that ageism
was the major problem and suggested that it was getting worse:

> Employers assume that older people want more money. When we first started in
> 1983 we used to help what we classed as the older unemployed which was 50-

55 plus. Now it's 35 plus and in reality that's 25 plus. There was an ad' in the paper that said the applicant should be mature with experience but then said the ideal age would be 24-26.

An adult education provider who ran pre-vocational training courses under the Training for Work scheme said:

There are people who we know who have been on our course who are 59, we're allowed to take people up to 63, the course in theory is for 18 - 63, but there are men of 59 who are being hassled into finding work. Even if they've got all the skills, all the personal skills and everything that's required of them, most employers want somebody who they can get more than six years work out of.

Another external constraint was that of residential prejudice on the part of employers, or 'postcodeism' as it was referred to by some key workers. This was where employers were seen to discriminate against individuals living in particular areas, usually stigmatised housing estates. The emphasis placed on postcodeism varied between areas and according to who was claiming its existence. Despite the difficulty of proving the existence of postcodeism some professionals advised their clients to disguise their addresses on CVs and application forms. The term 'postcodeism' is misleading since it was often the case that the postcode was used in preference to the name of an area as a means of camouflage. A training provider in one area said:

It's well known in this area. If you live in [X] that's a nice part, but if you live in [Y] you're a thief. I often tell clients to leave out (the name of the area) on an application form because someone from the other side of (the city) would know that, but they might not recognise (the postcode).

Racism and discrimination was also cited as a barrier to employment in one area where it was related to postcodeism. The area in question has a highly concentrated and diverse ethnic minority population and those inhabitants seeking work outside of the area were advised by one key worker to use the postcode. The name of the area was considered to be 'the kiss of death' on an application form. When focus group participants from this area were asked about barriers some of them stressed that racism and discrimination was a significant factor.

Employers' attitudes towards long-term unemployed people generally were often said to be suspicious and negative. Some focus group participants felt that they were stigmatised by employers merely by virtue of being unemployed for a long period:

They think that there must be something wrong if you've been out of work for quite a while. They get into a mind-set, there's an assumption that there must be something wrong with you.

If you're in a job already, you're more likely to get another one. But if you've been unemployed for a certain time, employers won't look at you.

They're very cynical

An ES Adviser corroborated these views:

> There are so many answers to this question. I mean there are lots of prejudices on the part of employers who make assumptions about people who haven't been in work even though half the register, for example, have been unemployed for six months, it's still difficult to convince employers that that length of unemployment is normal and acceptable, a normal time for people to have between jobs these days. The long term unemployed become perceived as unemployable by employers.

A support worker in an employment access centre said that she had spent a lot of time, with varying degrees of success, trying to "educate" employers away from the notion that because someone had been unemployed for over six months there must be something wrong with them:

> There's no doubt, as far as employers are concerned, that if you've been unemployed for more than six months, then there's definitely something wrong. This is the vision that employers have. And it's going to take a lot of work to get them away from that, and to get them to realise that the first six months shoots past, and it's only when you're a year unemployed that you suddenly realise, you know, "oh my god, what's happened, I should have taken more action sooner".

A few providers mentioned the problems faced by those unemployed people with criminal records, and the significant barriers that this created. One focus group participant was particularly angry at having been dismissed from a local authority job in child care because (he claimed) they had changed their policy on employing people with previous convictions:

> I'm unemployed due to poor management. I was given a job and after six weeks of running this place, they decided, because of my previous convictions, that I shouldn't be given the post. Actually they were spent convictions and I did declare them, that's why it was down to poor management because if it was going to be a problem, they never should have even short listed me for the post, let alone leave me to run it for six weeks...What's going on now, right, as I'm researching more and more into the job market, is that I'm finding a lot more barriers clamping down, whatever they may be, once they do police checks, it can be for shoplifting at the age of twelve, whereas before they would look at the nature of the offence and say "Well, that doesn't have any effect upon his performance or attitude", [now] they're not even considering you anymore.

Personal characteristics

A number of key workers stressed that the personal characteristics of the clients they worked with acted as barriers to employment. Some of these qualities were perceived as inherent to particular individuals, or groups of individuals, whilst others were said to arise from the experience of being unemployed. For example, some key workers argued that extended periods of unemployment gave rise to psychological barriers. A provider of adult numeracy and literacy courses said:

Welfare-to-work and the long term unemployed

A lot of the people we see…it's so long since they worked…they're frightened of the uncertainty…they've survived on benefits this long so why take the risk?

The manager of an employment access centre in another area was quite emphatic that fear and uncertainty was the major hurdle for all involved:

Fear!…absolute abject terror. It's fear by the employers. "This person hasn't worked for X amount of time, why haven't they? what's wrong with them?" Fear from the unemployed person in that, "I've applied for all these jobs, I've been rejected so what's wrong with me". And then all of a sudden they get offered a job, and it's a case of, "what happens if it doesn't work? what happens if I make a mistake?"

One focus group participant described how anxiety inhibited his prospects of getting the kind of work he was seeking:

I get anxious in interviews. If they're interviewing ten people for a job, the interviewer is going to select the best person at "doing" interviews, not necessarily the best in their ability to actually do the job…that's a problem I've personally experienced.

A project manager in one area described in some detail how he had developed voluntary training courses with the aid of European funding aimed at tackling what he perceived as the psychologically damaging effects of long periods of unemployment:

We identified a group of people whose needs weren't being met by existing training schemes. They were a group who would drop out of existing schemes quite easily, they were de-motivated, lacking confidence, had settled into unhealthy routines, that sort of thing. We developed a training course for long term unemployed people to rebuild confidence and motivation…developing what employers call 'soft skills' which is about stickability, reliability, team work, building up confidence, communication skills, all those sort of things which effectively bar employment and are quite significant areas where people can become de-skilled when they're unemployed for a long period of time. We were keen not to duplicate anything that was already in existence, there was nothing around in (this area) that was tackling this issue. Everything was vocationally oriented around specific jobs, and there was specific training going on, but people were coming out with no jobs to go into and it was just the cycle of things. What we wanted to do was to give people something that would sustain them and give them personal, empowering skills that would help them in terms of the choices they made and also give them a sense of value about themselves that was not related to work, although obviously the courses have an employment focus in terms of things like developing interview skills and making career choices.

A provider of ES programmes in another area explained that, as the unemployment register was falling, he was coming across increasing numbers of people exhibiting similar characteristics to those referred to above. He intimated that existing ES provision was not capable of meeting the needs of such people:

> *Jobclubs have failed miserably over the last two years to achieve targets(Five years ago there was a good crop of unemployed people out there.. who were employable... It's the other way round now. Because the people we have, unfortunately, are the people who have real problems. Not the unemployable, not the people who are not employed because they don't want to be, although they're always going to be out there, nor the people who are unemployed because they just need a CV, but there's people out there who are unemployed because they cannot physically hold down a job in terms of literacy, numeracy, timekeeping ability, concentration, whatever. And that's the difference.*

A Jobclub leader in another area made some similar observations and argued that employers expectations were unrealistic:

> *The people that are left on the register now, most of them are coming to be long term unemployed. These are the people that you're going to find it really hard to get into work. But employers still think they're going to get Action Man and Barbie (Doll), but they're not. The people that you're left with are not your budding, super-positive, charismatic people.*

A provider of adult numeracy and literacy suggested that the employment prospects for people with low ability were bleak, particularly when linked to age:

> *We've been saying for quite a while that there are no jobs for the people of a very low ability level... Some of those people have other skills, I mean we had one man on this programme who falls into the category I've just described, he can barely read and write. But he has done lots of jobs and he's obviously employable but he can't get over that hurdle of becoming employed. As he's getting older that is getting more and more difficult for him.*

The benefits trap

Another significant barrier to employment was the 'benefits trap', where potential earnings are either at, near or below total benefit levels. Some people we spoke to considered the benefits trap to be a major barrier to employment, others emphasised it less. Some people felt it was a legitimate barrier, others did not. For many focus group participants the benefits trap was a significant and legitimate barrier and was less a matter of choice than of simple economics:

> *I think most people are just stuck in the benefits trap. In (this area) there's not much Council accommodation with low rent, so most people are having to pay*

landlords £65, £75 or £85 a week rent, you know what I mean, plus you're getting your £45 dole and the jobs to earn £120 don't come nowhere near it.

There's an agency up the road and there's a sign for Food Processing .. £3.25 an hour and that's reasonably well paid, especially if you go into some residential homes or things like that.... but if you're paying £65 a week rent, which the Council would be paying and if you add on to that the Council Tax that you'd be liable for, and opticians and prescription charges... so it's a financial reason that you can't afford to work unless you're lucky enough to get one of the decent jobs.

It gets us back to this guy saying this thing about no restrictions, they're forcing you to take that job, put yourself on a lower rate than Income support or else "we're going to stop your money" and they're allowed to do it. It wouldn't be so bad if it was a job where you had decent money where you can cope but you've got a job with horrible money, very low money, and you've also got a job that you're not going to be happy with so you're not giving the employer your full potential, are you? And in effect you'll be on Family Credit or something anyway so you're sponging off the state anyway. OK you're not signing on as unemployed but you're still getting benefit cheques.

Low pay is a problem. I mean it's OK for young people living at home with their parents, with low rent, like it's not good. They [employers] shouldn't get away with paying low wages. You should get what you're worth. But for an older person who's away from home, like me, I'm fifty four with my own flat with Council Tax and all that, it's very difficult to survive on a low wage.

I think that the Government doesn't do enough to put pressure on employers. They [employers] know that an adult cannot live on the kind of money they're offering and, you know, adults are probably more reliable than the average school leaver who are probably thinking about everything but work!

Key workers' opinions on this issue were more varied but most of them felt that for the people they came across the attitudes were realistic and legitimate. A group of Restart and Jobplan Workshop providers asked about barriers to employment said:

For the clients we deal with its the pay levels that are out there, they're sort of caught in the benefits trap. If they take up work they're not going to get enough for housing etc. That's the main thing (endorsed by colleagues). Also age, they feel that they're over the hill at 35. Those are the two main things.

Asked whether they thought that their clients' were realistic about their wage expectations a colleague replied:

They're very cynical

Definitely, yes. I mean they're not asking for too much. The people that come on to these courses don't exaggerate. They're asking for a reasonable wage to live on. A married person for example would ask for about £300 per week which isn't a lot.

The first respondent added:

You have to bear in mind the average rent in London is about £100; £75 minimum, £100 is normal, and anything up to £150-200 is what they're paying. So that's determining the salary levels they're asking for.

An ES Adviser who had previously talked about the negative attitudes of employers added that:

There are things on the part of the clients themselves. Obviously financial considerations. People become benefit-dependent in a way, in the sense that they get their Giro every week, they get their Housing Benefit paid, and it becomes quite comfortable in a way, and to move to a job where things are all going to be disrupted again is, sort of, uninviting.

Part-time work, temporary work and in-work benefits

We wanted to find out what long term unemployed people's attitudes were towards doing part-time or temporary work and whether or not they had done any. A few focus group participants had done some part time work during their period of unemployment but their experiences of negotiating the benefits system had deterred them from doing it again. Some people argued that although there were social and psychological benefits to taking part time work these were outweighed by what they saw as the financial disincentives to doing it:

They could have grades of Unemployment Benefit to encourage people to do part-time work because that's the only way really that you'll ever get into full-time work and find those opportunities. If you look at the (paper).. you'll find that a lot of jobs are part-time, far more than full-time. OK they're not brilliantly paid but there are a lot of them - in restaurants, shops, pubs. You could be encouraged to do something like that without thinking "well, I'll actually only earn a fiver." And taking part-time work would make you look better in the eyes of a prospective employer because your present employer could give you a reference and show that you had recent experience and were a willing worker.

The system makes it bad for those little bits of work that you pick up here and there. And you need those little bits to introduce you to people and opportunities. If the system was reformed to accommodate part-time work then a lot more people would do it because there are far more part-time jobs around than full-time jobs and you could pick up new skills on them. Say, like if you earned under £50 you wouldn't lose anything then you'd do it and declare it. It'd be an incentive because you've got to pay rent, you've got to buy food, you've got to

Welfare-to-work and the long term unemployed

pay bills so you don't want to lose benefits for such little money. Your dole doesn't go for any of that, you dole is keeping you alive.

One focus group member claimed that he had been financially disadvantaged for taking up part time work in the past:

I did work part-time last year for six months but what happened was, although I was on minimum hours, I was earning £40 a week, I went on to Family Credit which was supposed, in theory, to bump up my income, but in the end I ended up losing about £40 a week... So it's a Catch-22.

A common complaint from focus group participants who had done part time work was that it disrupted their claim which meant a lot of additional paper work. Apart from the inconvenience this sometimes caused problems of continuity when they went back to sign on once the employment had ended:

Another problem is when you've taken up part-time work and then when it ends trying to get your benefits sorted. You have to answer a great big list of questions. There definitely should be some sort of leeway. I mean they have all your details on file and it's obvious from the type of job that you're taking that it's only going to be a temporary position, like at the Post Office for Christmas, so why have you got to wait to get your benefits? It takes a least a month, more like two... It's the same with the Council as well. If they're paying your rent and then you've got a job, they stop it [Housing Benefit]. You go back in January or February, whenever your short-term contract ends, it's the same, it's a new claim. It takes you about three weeks, going in several times a week, to straighten it all out, to tell them that you're not eligible to pay the Council Tax and to stop sending you letters about it. It's like talking to a brick wall.

Even if you're on part-time work you do have to pay for accommodation, council charge, health charges etc...plus, like if you do one day extra, you have to go and fill in all these forms out again so the next week you're not doing that day so you've to fill in all the forms again. And then as soon as you start working part-time you get the Fraud Squad on you, well I've not had that personally but I know people that have.

For some focus group participants the disruption to JSA claim continuity meant associated problems with claims for Housing Benefit and Council Tax. The fear of losing Housing Benefit, with the associated fear of homelessness, was enough to deter some people from even considering taking part time work:

If you sign off, you lose your benefits, your credits, you have to pay your Community Charge and if you're not earning enough then you have to claim all the other benefits. It's complicated and it takes a lot of time as they have to put you through again. You have to put in a new claim for your Housing Benefit and everything. And then when you go back, when the job is finished and sign on again to claim everything that you claimed while you were unemployed, that takes time and you end up with the landlord on your back and what have you. And that time when you sign on is the time at which you start being unemployed again, you're new again. So it's a lot of hassle.

One focus group participant's comments summarised the views of many others on this issue by saying:

The process itself is not what I call sustaining. It doesn't help you move from one step to the next, to a full-time situation to maintain an even amount coming in. It would be a better thing if they could simplify the whole thing, all the benefits.

With regard to in-work benefits such as Family Credit, very few focus group participants had any substantive comments to make other than those quoted. Some key workers however had received feedback from their clients about in-work benefits. A provider of Restart and Jobplan Workshop courses said:

We pass on information. We tell them they can get extra benefits whilst they're still working etc, but then they come up with comments like "when I'm working I don't want to have anything to do with the ES, I want to stay away from them, why should I, whilst I'm working, why should I still apply for benefits, why should I have to go through that hassle again, why should I have to 'review my progress' every six months. I don't want to do that, I want to stay away from the ES... That's the kind of comments we get. Also, not many people have heard of it. And that really only applies to people who are in a family environment because if you're a single person the in-work benefits mean nothing to you because you can't get anything out of it."

One ES Adviser made similar observations regarding in-work benefits but also alluded to abuse of the system by employers:

They can be an incentive but I think that what most people want at the end of the day is a wage-packet that they can take home and pay their bills from and not worry about a bit of Housing Benefit here, a bit of Family Credit there. They just want a wage to meet their outgoings. But I think that helps a lot of people. Again, Family Credit can be seen as a subsidy to employers. Actually, in the past I've had employers speak to me about what was the lowest rate that they could get away with paying somebody and still make sure that that person's not going

Welfare-to-work and the long term unemployed

to lose out. So they sort of shape the wage to fit in with the benefits culture, if you like. I don't think that happens a lot.

Most focus group participants claimed to know little, if anything, about in-work benefits. The ES Adviser quoted above offered one explanation for this lack of awareness:

Another thing about in-work benefits is that because there are so many of these different things that people can claim while they're working and they've all got different eligibility criteria, you know, to start, to actually get a handle on it is very difficult, to get the expertise in it. So, for example, they brought out extended Housing Benefit about last October, so people can carry on getting their Housing Benefit for the first four weeks when they start work, but staff know so little about it. So you get loads of people coming in saying, "I was never told about it, I didn't know, why didn't you tell me?"

Yet some ES frontline people in another area claimed that significant numbers of claimants were making increasing use of Family Credit to top up low wages. They did however suggest that in-work benefit calculations were time-consuming and that consequently less use was made of them than otherwise could be:

We do get quite a lot of queries about Family Credit but we tend to use it more as a selling point to them. Mainly it crops up when you're doing a job search with someone, especially long-term unemployed. There are quite a lot of clients who are sort of in the benefit trap and they'll say, "oh I can't work for less than £300 per week", but they're totally unskilled. And when you go into the system and do a job search for £300 or more all the jobs are fully skilled sort of things. So then you have to start using the "have you got children, Housing Benefit, Council Tax, did you know that you can get help".

There is quite a bit of take-up but it's difficult because you've only got seven minutes with the person so you tend then to have to refer it to the Advisers who have actually got the in-work benefit calculation on LMS so they can actually do print outs. It is difficult when you've got somebody in front of you. They can say "oh I can't accept that it's not enough" and you're very much working in the dark. Actually doing an in-work benefit calculation from start to finish, you're talking about at least twenty minutes. Because you have to put everything in. How much Housing Benefit they're on, how many children, savings, whatever. In terms of the multi-functionality of people in Jobcentres there's only certain people who really know about in-work benefits to any great extent...The interesting thing is when employers start quoting it to you as well but that's another issue about wages.

T he ES is the primary government agency responsible for assisting the long-term unemployed into work. Not only does it provide services itself, it also occupies a key position between unemployed people and all the other various agencies and organisations who provide services for unemployed people. Firstly, we wanted to know what long term unemployed people felt about the quality of service provided by the ES. Secondly, given the strategic role of the ES, we wanted to learn about its co-ordinating role between long term unemployed claimants and other provider organisations.

The views of the long term unemployed

The findings from the focus groups indicate that, in general, long term unemployed people had a very critical view of the ES in terms of its ability to help them find work, or guide them through the variety of initiatives aimed at helping them improve their employability. Criticisms tended to be directed very much towards the organisational level rather than at particular individuals. Similar attitudes were also apparent during the interviews with key workers in other organisations. There was a strong overall sense that ES staff had a difficult job to do but that it was made even more difficult through a lack of resources, compounded in some cases by poor management. The ES staff we spoke to consistently referred to the lack of time available to spend with clients in order to provide effective guidance and assistance. Morale amongst ES staff was said to be very low and this was manifest in high staff turnover, particularly over the previous two years, especially amongst more junior grades who had most day-to-day contact with the unemployed. According to many key workers, high staff turnover was a major problem where it had implications for the continuity of working relationships, both between the ES and the unemployed, and between the ES and provider organisations. In particular, the loss of experienced staff was thought to be particularly detrimental, as was the increased use of inexperienced casual workers to fulfil front line duties.

Focus group participants' perception of the ES in general was that it was a badly run organisation. There were three main criticisms of the ES in terms of its ability to help them improve their employment prospects. The first and most prominent criticism was that ES staff did not seem to have enough time to deal with them as individuals:

> I worked for 25 years and then I was made redundant .. I went for my interview and I was thinking "What's going on here?" No one made even the slightest attempt to motivate me. There was no going through what I wanted to do. Did I want to change my work? Nothing. It's like a production line. You go in, you're

out with nothing in between to help you. I found the staff very amicable, nice people, but whether they don't have the time or the training or what, they just leave you on your own... I was back in the job market after 25 years without a day unemployed in my life and I hadn't got a clue about anything. No one told me about benefits, or the Council Tax, nobody told me about anything at all. I found out, but I had to find out by myself.

I'd like it sometimes if someone would just sit down and talk to me personally.

The theory is that at the Jobcentre you at least have the chance to talk to some-body. That's the theory, but it never works.

They [Jobcentre staff] have skills when dealing with the public, they're polite and all the rest of it but that was in one particular office. I've had experiences in the past when they've been less polite. But, at the same time, it was very rushed. You have to fill in that form [the JSAg] within a certain amount of time and if it's not filled in you have to come back tomorrow. So a lot of bureaucracy. ... They're not organised or they haven't got the manpower, whatever the reason.

There's no one in the Jobcentre who will spend time with you.

The second major criticism from focus group participants was that they felt as though the primary function of the ES was to try to remove them from the unemployment register rather than to provide genuine help:

Their [ES Staff] training is in how to deal with people who are unemployed, not in how to get people back into employment. It's just to get you off the register somehow.

The Careers Service should be doing it. They are the right person for the job, so to speak, because they can discuss which options are open to you but the ES are there to get you off the bloody figures. That's the difference in attitude. They can't sit down and help you with guidance into your options, they have no one to give you advice.

It all comes down to attitude. They look at you as if their job is to stop you fiddling; they're not there to offer a service. They're there to stop you ripping off the system not to actually provide you with what you need. Their attitude is that they're there to do a job and that job is to get them signed on and off.

The perception that the primary function of the ES was to remove people from the unemployment register was often backed up by reference to the achievement of performance targets:

The Careers Service generally has a positive view of things while the Jobcentre has a negative view of the same situation. One is a restrictive view while the other is a progressive sort of thing. In theory, the Jobcentre should know about the labour market and how to help you but in reality they don't. It's all back to figures. Get you off the dole, get your name off the list, "that's another one, knock it off". They have to meet their targets, they don't care where you go because if you come back in six months time you're not the same figure, you're a new one.

The feeling I get a lot of the time is that the people there want a tick [to show] that they've done something. They're not really interested whether you're getting a bloody job or not, all they want are a few ticks because they are under pressure to get results.

The third major criticism of the ES from focus group participants, which has already been alluded to, was the perception that staff lacked sufficient knowledge and experience to be able to help them:

They ask specific questions like "What jobs have you had?", "How long have you been unemployed?", "What qualifications have you got?" So then they can say, "You're in this box", "You're in that box", but they don't actually talk things through with you. You need someone who knows what you're talking about and can put you on the right track.

I went into my place [Jobcentre] and said that I wanted to know where my local Jobclub was and nobody moved. They just kept sending me from desk to desk. One guy was looking through his desk saying "Oh, I know it's somewhere, there is one." That was the kind of response I got and then finally a lady told me about this place [a voluntarily run employment access and training centre] and she said to me "Let me know what it's like after you've been." And I just thought, you know, what kind of service is this? These people are supposed to be encouraging us to find work or helping us and they didn't even know where the Job Club was!

One focus group participant explained his personal strategy for dealing with what he perceived as intrusive and unnecessary review interviews, by capitalising on their inexperience and lack of knowledge:

When you get experienced, you can really wind them up, have them running round and round in circles. And if you go there for an interview, the thing to do is don't let them come at you, you go at them. Don't just let them ask you things, you've got to do the asking. After you've rabbited away for about half an hour, they'll say "Well, goodbye" and be glad to get rid of you!

Welfare-to-work and the long term unemployed

Some focus group participants who were critical of the ES as an organisation were keen to point out that they did not blame individual staff members. They clearly felt that the negative attitudes of staff towards claimants were a reflection of staff attitudes towards their jobs.

There's a real attitude there towards you. I know someone who works there and she has changed. I've known her a long time...she hates going into work...she's always miserable and fed up and that attitude is definitely put on to us.

Yeah a lot of the staff in the Jobcentre are on short-term contracts and the wages are not very high and they sit behind the counter with a laid-back attitude. They don't have the motivation, they just do what the system requires though different Jobcentres probably have different attitudes.

When I go to sign on and talk with my Employment Adviser they're constantly being negative about my situation and I tell them "Look compared to what you've said, I'm probably the most positive person in this office right now". Their eyes glaze over and that is it, you get absolutely nowhere.

One focus group participant offered his vision of how the ES ought to operate:

As soon as you sign on you have an interview and that person you see then could act as a careers adviser and that sort of person would know how to guide you. For example, they would know what professions weren't taking people on at that time and which were because at forty five you need to know which ones are useful. That would be a better set-up than just having somebody sitting at a desk who has a lot of other people to see and just says to you "Have you applied for two jobs? Yes, well that's fine, bye." Because that's not really constructive, that's just a check on you before they let you have your money.

A fellow focus group participant however was adamant that he would not regard the ES as a useful source of careers advice regardless of any changes they may make in the future:

With my past experiences, if I was to go into the Jobcentre and it was all new and they had a desk with Careers on it, I wouldn't give them the benefit of the doubt. New people, new training, new image, none of it would make me try it again.

The views of key workers

Most of the providers we spoke to were also quite critical of the ES as an organisation. The bulk of providers' criticisms stemmed from the issue of high staff turnover that had several implications. Firstly, it meant that there was an increasing tendency within the ES to employ casual workers on temporary contracts. A provider of numeracy and literacy courses described the situation in her area:

over the last five or six years since I've attended the Jobcentre on a regular basis. I've found that the permanent staff are all moving back, away from the frontline, doing much more 1-2-1 counselling or specific jobs which are probably much more satisfying. But people on the frontline, on the whole, are the people on short-term contracts, very young, kids in there twenties, who have been given appalling jobs to do.

The manager of a voluntary employment access centre in another area had formerly been a provider of ES programmes. He recounted his experiences of working with the local office:

The Claimant Advisers were turning over so quickly, either being promoted or dropping out or going off sick. Anybody that's any good on the frontline is moved upstairs, anybody that's not doing too well is left to get on with it. A lot of the staff at the local office were temps, for a long time. Then the funding for that dried up. So the staff are having to do twice as much work, for the same amount of money, getting twice as much aggravation because they're always changing the rules, and they're going off sick...and they can't replace them. The money they're paid, it's not worth it. The local office lost at least four of their really good staff to recruitment agencies. They're not getting so much grief because people come to you because they want to come to you, and you're actually getting results and getting paid for it as well.

The issue of ES staff working on short-term contracts had not gone unnoticed by claimants. According to one focus group participant there were clear implications for the standard of service available:

And they're reducing the number of staff in there so they think "I might be out of work in six months time". They're obviously anxious about their security and future and I don't think they feel good about their jobs because in their hearts they know they can't do much to help us.

A training provider deplored the lack of experienced front line ES staff:

It's very easy to knock the staff at the ES but they have a very difficult job and they're tied down by all sorts of rules and regulations. And they're working with a skeleton staff of very unqualified, untrained people and largely people who've come through on three or six month contracts, so they're constantly re-training...it's appalling.

One direct consequence of having inexperienced staff on the front line was that the quality of the advice and guidance that the ES was able to offer long term unemployed people on a day-to-day basis could be poor and sometimes inaccurate. One training provider was quite candid about this issue:

The sad thing is...the girls, the boys on the front desk, and this is going to sound really derogatory, kids, they don't know the first thing about their own jobs let alone about vacancies.

Although some providers recounted anecdotes about individuals whom they felt were particularly unhelpful, most had developed strong working relationships with one or two key personnel in specific ES offices. These relationships were said to be invaluable in sorting out difficulties with the benefit regulations concerning attendance on voluntary training and education courses. However, these connections could be fragile, especially with high ES staff turnover. A training provider explained how high staff turnover not only made his own job more difficult, but also had damaging consequences for claimants when ES staff gave out incorrect information regarding part time study:

> *I get one of these problems [16 hour] now about every few weeks. However if an office changes staff... There was suddenly an influx of problems from this one office because they'd got new staff in who were mostly temps, who'd been given a basic..."this is the system, these are the rules". The problem is that when they're [claimants] threatened with losing their benefits they leave the course and that is what we're trying to stop. It's ok for me, I'm educated. I can sort it out. But a claimant who quite possibly isn't so well educated and doesn't have access to the information...? I've got a standard response now for Benefit Officers because I got so fed up with doing it. I just refer them to the relevant paragraphs of the JSA regulations. I got the information from experienced Client Advisers who were actually very helpful; it's just that I had to go through four people to get there. Some are co-operative others aren't so.*

High staff turnover was also perceived to be damaging to the relationship between the ES and claimants due to the lack of continuity. A training provider argued that continuity was an important factor in developing constructive relationships with clients:

> *There's no continuity at all in the Jobcentre. We know our clients and they trust us. We listen to the unemployed, we listen to the issues...and they don't.*

The issue of continuity was deemed important not just by providers but also by some focus group participants:

> *Yeah, instead of seeing different people each time you sign on, or seeing different people about particular adverts, it might be better if you had a careers adviser who you could see privately in an office and they could look at what you are capable of doing and say "Have you thought about this?" or "Have you thought about that?"*

Some providers were former ES employees who had moved job partly because they felt frustrated at not being able to offer the sort of help they felt people needed. A Jobclub leader in one area who had worked for the ES for three and a half years gave his reasons for leaving:

> *Everything in the ES is directed. The law says this, let's do it, bang! There's no common sense; there's no living in the real world. Because the book says this,*

you do it. It's pathetic. I was collecting written warnings like people collect book matches. I used to have queues of people come into the Jobcentre and ask for me by name because they knew that I wouldn't give them any bullshit. So the order came down that from now on you can only spend five minutes with a client. I said "you can't do that, every person's complaints are different". They said, "your not here to deal with complaints, you're here to deal with benefits." That to me was unacceptable and so I started doing things my way and the ES didn't like it. So in the end I had to resign because we were just fighting each other.

The views of ES staff

When we asked existing ES staff about their work they validated many of the criticisms made by focus group participants and other key workers. All agreed that staff turnover had increased and that it was sometimes problematic. One member of staff suggested that this was a recent phenomenon:

You tend to find that the people that are in the Jobcentres have been there for quite a few years now but they are leaving. Just the other week somebody who had been there for six years turned round and said, "I've got another job." There's a lot of people threatening to leave all the time, you know, "I've had enough of this" but I think it's been more noticeable recently. It's quite a timely thing, suddenly people are starting to drift away you know.

When existing ES staff were asked why they thought people were leaving the replies tended to centre on notions of fatigue, stress and burnout:

It's getting to a point now where there's like a sort of depression that's going through all the front line staff because you suddenly realise that this is it, this is what I'm going to be doing now until whenever…and it's literally like being on a production line, mind numbingly boring, because you're just kind of, client after client after client. On my section, because it's the two year plus [unemployed] you're constantly pushing, all the time, you know well, "Did you phone that employer last week? Well why? Well have you tried this?" "What about changing in a different direction and looking at this?".. All the time, pushing, and I can see there's going to be burnout.

They used to have a thing with the old style Restart interviews called Adviser Burnout where basically you just see these people and you're battling away against a brick wall and you just get burnt out with it. I've seen it very recently actually. The people on the front line on the long term unemployed sections where you're dealing with people, there's a lot of them, you know, that have a lot of problems for various reasons, you get a lot of aggression, you get care in

Welfare-to-work and the long term unemployed

the community cases, but people do get worn down by them. I've seen people get worn down by it, and, you know, just shot away with the job, because they're interviewing all the time, and they're just shot away with it.

All the ES staff we spoke to were experienced, full time employees yet even within this group the question of inexperience was still an issue. One member of staff explained how she had been transferred to a different field of work dealing with the public with no training:

I'm from the old benefit type Jobcentre, whereas I used to do the benefit side of things, processing claims etc., and really like the Jobcentre work, you know the labour market stuff, I'm only really new to .. being thrown in, you know, front line, and you know, "this is your terminal, right, get on with it" with like no sort of labour market knowledge at all.

ES staff claimed that the biggest impediment to doing their job properly was a lack of sufficient time to spend with individual clients. Closely allied to this was the pressure to meet performance targets. One ES frontline worker explained what she had to think about in the seven minutes that were allocated to each client in her office:

At the moment it's all placements, placements, placements, you're alright... don't worry about the programmes, just placings, and then suddenly the District's figures on programmes have dipped. The referrals have gone up as far as placements are concerned but the actual programmes have started to fall, so now it's a panic: "oh you've got to start submitting people to Jobclub or Training for Work". But you've still got to get your placings. So when you're on frontline there's so many things that are going through your head, you've got someone in front of you and you're sort of thinking, now, ooh, perhaps Training for Work, no, perhaps Jobclub, ooh, no, no, no, I think maybe they need pre-vocational training and it's literally like, you need a sort of prompt beside you. And then someone will say something like "what's happened about mortgage interest payments?" And you're like, "eh, what?" And if you've got a client sitting in front of you and you're thinking about trying to sell them Family Credit or something, you can imagine all the questions they're going to ask, like "well I want something that's permanent, and I want something that's going to be paying this", you know, you can just picture the questions they're going to ask and you think, it's just not worth it. And all this in seven minutes.

Some ES staff clearly felt that the pressure to meet performance targets prevented a client centred approach to their work.

If you want to do the very best for the client that's sitting in front of you you've got to take away the being driven by targets. At the end of the day, instead of thinking, right, what's the best thing for this client, you're thinking like, hmm, perhaps I could get this client on Training for Work, which is wrong.

Targets become an end in themselves. It's not about 'this will help somebody' it's about 'it's a target'. We've just got to get certain numbers on a particular scheme. At the moment it's happening with our placements. We've got this six-point plan. They know for definite that we're not going to get our APA on placings so they've drawn up this six point plan for October and for the rest of the year which basically says you must try and refer every person that comes through the door to a job. So the submission rate goes up but the submission to placement ratio goes through the roof.

The ES has got to decide whether it's a business or an ES. It's not really an ES now it's more of a business. The idea of a service for people that come in, because of numerical targets, has gone by the board to a large extent. I mean yes, there is an element of that [service] but that's largely down to the good will of the people that work there.

Another issue that was referred to by providers and ES staff was the notion of role conflict whereby frontline staff were expected to provide help to clients whilst at the same time ensure that they were complying with the benefit regulations. One Claimant Adviser put it this way:

The ES believes that you can be things with two heads really. You can be Mr Nasty - "if you don't do this I'll stop your benefits blah, blah, blah" - and then Mr helpful. But I think the two things are in conflict more than the ES believes they are.

The notion of role conflict was also linked to the issue of performance targets. A training provider was quite emphatic that the two roles were incompatible:

I think there's a blatant conflict of interests. Someone who is there as a Client Adviser who is implicitly there to help you into work cannot at the same time have targets for referring you to Adjudication.

Another training pointed out that staff at one of his local Jobcentres were unwilling to perform the benefit policing role with any degree of commitment. It was not deemed to be in their own interests to do so, nor was it thought to be beneficial to the long-term interests of their clients.

They know very well that they've got more people on the books than they've got jobs to offer them and that they're not going to just use a strict regime to force people out onto jobs. They'd rather support people and refer them onto things that are going to help them long-term. They know very well that it's not going to help their performance targets and they're going to get flack for it. And they've made, probably, an unofficial decision that given the choice between reaching their targets or helping people, if they go for their targets they're likely to get thumped in the face and fail on their targets, whereas if they go for helping people then they're more likely to achieve their targets in terms of help-ing people to obtain work.

Welfare-to-work and the long term unemployed

There was a great deal of confusion among focus group participants regarding the names, nature and purpose of different ES schemes and programmes. This confusion was most manifest when they were asked specifically about those programmes where attendance is mandatory. For example, a common misunderstanding concerned the status of Jobclub, which many participants thought were compulsory. Adding to the general confusion was the proliferation of Jobclub type activities and services often run by voluntary organisations to which some claimants had been referred by ES staff. Consequently discussants would often use the term 'Jobclub' as a generic term when referring to either a drop-in centre or an employment access centre run by a voluntary organisation, an official Jobclub, or a Jobplan Workshop. The following sections, however, focus on official ES programmes, albeit that most were run by various external agencies under contract to the ES.

Compulsory courses: Jobplan and Restart

The vast majority of focus group participants who expressed an opinion felt that compulsory attendance on Jobplan Workshops or Restart Courses was a "complete waste of time". Questions about these courses were often greeted with derision usually expressed through laughter and the shaking of heads. Probing this issue would illicit comments such as the following:

It's a joke - Restart.

In the JobPlan Workshop, we were talking one day about the difficulty of getting to places without a car and one of the tutors said, "Oh, get a part-time job and you can save your £5 a week [to save up enough money to buy a car]", well, we all collapsed!

I've been to two Job Clubs and a Restart programme... The Jobclub is useful for the equipment that it offers - the computers and the newspapers. Restart is a problem. You have to go or else you'll lose your money. It would be better if it was voluntary.

I think that a lot of these schemes are run by people who are hired out to work aren't they. They're from private companies and they have nothing to do with being unemployed. They know nothing about it fundamentally and you get guys standing up there going "Come on then!", trying to raise your morale, you know,

*telling you to wear shoulder-pads and you know, power dress and go out there.
You don't want to be told this stuff.*

Although some ES Advisers could understand the negative attitude of claimants towards compulsory schemes any sympathy they may have had was tempered by the notion that there was always the chance that an individual "might learn something useful" and hence they had few qualms about referring claimants to these courses.

A major criticism of Jobplan and Restart from claimants was that the course content was too broad and not directly relevant to their particular circumstances. Some claimants also felt that course tutors were more concerned to achieve their targets than to consider what might be the most appropriate action for the individual. There was a general air of cynicism among focus group participants typified by the following observation:

I went to Jobplan Workshop and you go in there and you sit down and drink tea, basically. There's a lot more I can say but that's all you do, and at the end of the week you see the chief bloke and he puts you at the computer and he'll tap out what jobs you're suitable for. You're not going to get a job, but (they) can manipulate the figures better than Ladbrokes can and I'm not being funny,...like our friend said over there, they can get 2 million [unemployed] halved...or whatever they want, it's all statistics! Jobplan Workshop is a way of manipulating the figures.

The factual accuracy of the statements is largely irrelevant, it is the perceptions and action (or inaction) resulting from those perceptions that is important. If in areas of high unemployment such negative attitudes are widespread and deeply entrenched then it is going to be difficult to convince long-term unemployed claimants of the merits of any scheme.

Providers of these courses generally felt that the courses could be of more benefit if they (the providers) could have more input into the course content. At the time of the research, however, the courses had to be run in accordance with strict guidelines set out in the manuals provided by the ES:

The design of the programmes is not down to us at all. It comes down from on high, it's apparently researched and sorted out by psychologists... Very little changes once a programme's up and running. The programme for the Jobclub, for example, the eight or nine training sessions, hasn't changed since the year dot, ten years, since it came from America. So no, we have no influence on that.

Another provider was more openly critical about the content of the ES manuals:

There's a manual which we have to follow, it's designed by these psychiatrists [laughter from colleagues] who have never met these people but, er, have been doing things on theory, OK. But in practice it's different you know, when you start dealing with real people things are different you know.

All the current providers we spoke to felt that the courses, as presently structured, were too short and too generalised. One provider's comments summarise this view:

What you tend to get in these courses is a middle of the road, homogeneous mess which is good for everybody but not always necessarily good for the individual.

From a provider's perspective, this was a situation made worse by the fact that the ES did not screen referrals to courses. Consequently the diverse mix of people with widely differing needs and circumstances for any given intake made it difficult for the tutors to establish any meaningful rapport with the individuals in the group. Providers generally felt that the ES should be more selective about who they referred to courses.

A lot of the time, when we get people sent for these programmes, the truth is, many of the people that send the clients here have no idea what goes on in these programmes. They send the wrong type of people for our programmes. So whereas some we could help, for others, they're just spinning out time.

It could be that they just look at a programme, say like ours we're running here - "Jobplan Workshop starting in two weeks time, oh there's only fifteen people allocated to that, we've got to fill that up". And it could be that there's a big element of that, trying to fill up the groups with people who are not maybe entitled, or who have been before, so when they come back, "I didn't get help last time, I've been here before and nothing's been done" etc. .. Really and truly they shouldn't attend a Jobplan Workshop more than once. We do get a lot of clients who have been over and over again.

However one provider argued that any grading of referrals would be better handled by the providers themselves at programme centres (see Chapter 7) rather than by unqualified ES personnel at Jobcentres:

Multi-site centres are not good for the client... When you appear at the door you've already been designated a Jobclub client or a Restart client, ok, and you've been designated by, with respect, Claimant Advisers who are not trained counsellors, who are not training people, ok, and over a period of, I don't know how long, five to twenty minutes: they have (decided). The only reason they put you on a Restart Course is because you've reached two years. Or they put you on a Job search Plus or a Jobclub option because it's the least onerous option and it's the only one you're prepared to sign to say you'll take. And targets of course mean that there's a certain element of, you know, let's get the old jelly beans off the end of the factory line.

They're very cynical

This provider felt that the issue of selection was especially important in the case of those with literacy and numeracy problems where 'labelling' and 'stigmatising' at the Jobcentre could result in defensive and negative attitudes towards assistance. This provider had a dedicated literacy and numeracy unit on the premises and had been campaigning for the transition to programme centres whereby the ES referred all clients to the provider where they would be counselled and directed towards appropriate courses.

On the question of providers meeting the performance targets mandated by their ES contacts, the majority felt that although they were achievable, they were not always appropriate. The consensus among providers was that they were there to help people irrespective of performance targets. A typical response would be:

> Although we've got targets to meet, we don't consciously come into work everyday thinking we must reach our targets.

This provider went on to explain how it was sometimes difficult to place some clients and that it was not always possible to refer a client to what was considered best for them because it did not fall into the specified targets. In cases such as these heavy reliance was put on the "other" category on the list of target options although this could still be quite restrictive. When asked whether targets should be done away with however, one of this provider's colleagues was quite emphatic that they should not be:

> Simply because there are a large number of guys out there who are cowboys...and if you remove targets then as far as they're concerned it's open house and they can shove people in anywhere and get money.

This provider had been delivering Restart courses since their inception and had previously worked for other companies (one of which is still operating) whom he considered were less committed to providing genuine help. Although this provider was generally in favour of targets one of his colleagues was critical of the way that the ES kept changing them:

> They (the ES) tend to push different programmes at different times... ES might come down on their annual visit or every couple of months and say "you've had 50% in this category, we'd like you to up your intake on x category". So for the next however many months you try and push people through to another category. You're aware of the targets but you're not going to let them govern your life. As I said, basically we're here to help people so we try and help them as much as possible. And from that help, hopefully the targets will come out of that.

A former Restart tutor in another area who was made redundant in 1996 said that:

> If Restart was delivered well, there was a lot in it for people and people could get something at the end. .. The problem with it though was that towards the end of my time as a Restart tutor they started measuring the outcomes and so

Welfare-to-work and the long term unemployed

therefore your company would put a lot of pressure on you to comply with the outcomes.

Some current providers also commented that Jobplan and Restart could be marketed more positively instead of being used by the ES as a threat. These providers felt that much of the positive work that they were trying to do was undermined, not so much by the element of compulsion, but more by the way in which compulsion was used by the ES.

A former Restart tutor with five years experience was convinced that the ES referred people to compulsory courses whom they suspected of working in the informal economy.

The majority of focus group participants were, perhaps surprisingly, fairly ambivalent about the issue of compulsion per se. What they found annoying was that they were being compelled to do something that was, in their opinion, pointless:

> *I've been on a course where they talk about the CV and I found it a waste of time. I found that when you're there for a week, you could be out looking for work...you're wasting your time going for something that you already know and they force you to go otherwise you lose your money.*

> *I've stopped going on training now because training for what? There's no job at the end of it, so why bother? They can make you go on the schemes but I remember going on one and it wasn't anything related to finding a job, it was a Job Plan Workshop or something and the person who was doing it was not trained he could not help with the CV or anything. I had to go on it or I'd lose my benefit.*

> *My son didn't go on one and so he has lost his benefits. He didn't go because he had been on them before and he said "Dad, it's a load of rubbish."*

> *You just go in there and say "Yes sir, no sir" and listen to the waffle and then walk out the door. They're rubbish, nothing useful.*

On this issue a Restart provider commented:

> *People turn up on courses and say "I did CVs and interview skills and presentation skills three months ago on that course" and you say "tough!" You've got to do it again because it says so here, and you're mandatory. You've go to do it here, and if you don't come for every session on every day, we'll tell the Jobcentre and they'll cut your benefits.*

Another provider however said that he felt that no one should be made to go on more than one Restart or Jobplan Workshop:

They're very cynical

If it hasn't worked for them once, what is the point of making them go again and again? It can only cause problems and it's a waste of our time.

A training and education provider made a similar observation:

Something which is basically just putting a CV together then sending off for jobs, then another one, another one, another one. ... Well, they're just reinforcing the same patterns and same mistakes over and over again. If it didn't work last time then why should it work this time?

This provider said that he felt that some claimants needed encouragement but that compulsory attendance based on reaching a certain time period was ridiculous, particularly when it interrupted a longer training course or came two weeks after a more focused course which had covered the same ground more thoroughly and had been attended voluntarily.

Most focus group participants said that they attended these courses reluctantly and "played the game" in order to prevent the loss of benefit and "keep them (the ES) sweet". Some claimants however are apparently willing to risk the loss of a week's benefit by not attending. One of the larger companies providing these courses quoted the attendance figures for the region's previous six months. In one area there was an almost consistent non-attendance figure of 60% of referrals. Patterns of non-attendance are deemed consistent enough for the provider to over-recruit by the predicted shortfalls. None of the focus group participants said that they had deliberately not attended a compulsory course once they had been referred. A few claimants however did admit that they find the prospect of attending compulsory courses so "depressing" and/or "patronising" that they sought ways to avoid being referred in the first place. A popular method was to claim Sickness Benefit via a GP's certificate for a short period around the time of the JSA claim anniversary.

There is no way of knowing from this research how widespread such practices are and the ES advisers interviewed felt that this was a minor problem. However it does highlight yet another way in which the official statistics for both long-term unemployment and new claims are made inaccurate.

One focus group participant who spoke more positively about a Jobplan Workshop course she had attended said that she had found some of the information useful but that far more could have been achieved if the tutor hadn't had to spend so much time placating and arguing with other individuals in the group whom she felt were being deliberately disruptive:

I was on the Jobplan Workshop and I didn't mind but there were people there who were there because the Jobcentre said that if they didn't go they would stop their money. It might have been a better course than it was if you hadn't had people there who didn't want to be there... They spoilt it a little bit because the attitude and the atmosphere in there was poor.

An ex-provider who was highly praised by her former employer for her ability to exceed her targets for Restart, Jobplan Workshop and Jobclub had this to say about dealing with these potentially difficult situations:

> There was a lot of anger when people turned up for Restart. The people who run these things have their work cut out, especially on a Monday morning, people didn't want to be there and there was a lot of animosity, and I think the skill of the people who actually run these things has to be praised. To keep these people from actually wrecking the joint or, you know, throwing a punch here and there. I mean who wants to sit in a room full of people with BO, for two weeks, and be told, you know, you've got to do this or that?

Jobclubs

As mentioned earlier, there was a degree of confusion regarding the status of Jobclub which was evident during the focus group discussions where the term was often used to describe non-official Jobclub type activities. Official Jobclubs were generally felt by focus group participants to be the most useful of all ES programmes. Many focus group participants however had also experienced similar projects, variously described as employment access centres, drop-in centres, support groups and job clubs. These activities were usually run on a voluntary basis either by voluntary organisations, local authorities, TECs or various partnerships. In all cases where people had experienced official and non-official Jobclubs, the official ones compared unfavourably for a number of reasons.

The first criticism concerned the rules regarding access. Official Jobclub places are limited and under normal circumstances claimants can only join a Jobclub once they have been unemployed for six months. Some focus group participants felt that Jobclubs should be more accessible:

> If they were more accessible, you'd just go in there and use them, wouldn't you? Do your CV or use the phones or something like that and that'd be alright yeah? If they were more of a casual sort of a thing... But if you leave half way through, it could affect your benefit...if you have been made to go. Again, it's the entrenchment of the sides isn't it? It seems like a battle.

> I've been to Jobcentres and they've said "How long have you been unemployed? You have to be six months unemployed" and I think that's just ridiculous, you know. If you want a job and there's facilities there you should be able to use them. But everyone wants to keep you in their little groups, you're not allowed to step out of line and you're just trying to find a job, whatever it takes but those little things can really put people off.

Some focus group participants who were ineligible had tried to access official Jobclubs voluntarily and some claimed they had been successful. Jobclub leaders confirmed that this could happen and said they would accommodate people if they could but that it wasn't usually possible. Attendance still had to be sanctioned by the ES and relied ultimately on their discretion.

Another criticism made by some focus group participants was that Jobclub leaders were too keen to get claimants to apply for any work:

At the Jobclub, things are more formal. They have the attitude on the outside that they want to get you back into work and that they want to help you to do what you want to do but it doesn't feel like that. It feels like they want to get you off the register, get the statistics down, get you a job. Like when I've been in [the Jobclub] they didn't take much interest, they didn't say "Well, lets see if we can help you, get you a job related to your needs and abilities." They didn't really seem to care what I wanted.

You get people of all levels in there. At one Jobclub the woman there, if she didn't like the look of someone she used to get really horrible and people told me that she could be a right...one! She told people there to have ten job applications a day and if you didn't have those ten a day, she would tell the Unemployment Benefit and they'd stop the money then.

One official Jobclub leader claimed that he knew of a large commercial organisation in the local area that was also contracted to the ES to run Jobclubs. He explained that the organisation also ran a private recruitment agency and would often use unemployed claimants to fill temporary posts he referred to as "Christmas jobs". He felt that this was wrong and said that he would rather keep his clients at the Jobclub until they found a suitable full time permanent job.

Some focus group participants felt that official Jobclubs did not offer enough individual support:

It wasn't tailored, like, for anybody. You just came in and there was like loads of papers, there was loads of jobs that come in and, basically, you got some stamps. It was a Jobclub. And basically you had to sign on a register every day when you turned up and at the end of that week if they hadn't sent it off you wouldn't get paid. I didn't find it useful really. It did serve its purpose, like, it did give me stimulation to go on and look for other things and do what I wanted to do but there wasn't much support with it, basically it was some papers and that and free 'phones.

Some of the Jobclub frontline people have been very decent but some of the Jobclub leaders who have taken over, the power has gone to their... They just go in there and make life absolute hell. I think what it is, is some of them have the right qualifications but the wrong attitude. They assume that we don't want to work, that we're lazy bones, and these people just drive us further into the ground.

I think that they should break down the Jobclubs. ...have them split for different ages.

What appealed most to focus group participants about non-official job clubs was that they were flexible about attendance:

I've been to the Jobclub and it was helpful in so far as they gave you stamps and newspapers, the practical stuff, but they didn't actually give you a job. I also go once a week to an unemployment support group that's not run by the ES. It compares very well to the Jobclub actually. It's quite a relaxed atmosphere there because people are there basically because they want to be there, and it's voluntary. You can go there as and when it suits you, it's like a drop-in centre.

The difference between the Jobclubs and the group in the Community Centre is trust. With the Jobclubs, you've got to go through the ES, you know, and they give you a form and you've got to turn up and the Jobclub is a rigid structure [although] it might suit some people. It's hard to tell. The support group is a drop-in centre and its more trust, you know, so there's not the stipulation that you've got to write or 'phone up for X number of jobs. Also in the early days the Jobclubs used to, I don't know if they still do, vet the letters and allocate the stamps!

Half the staff in the Jobcentre haven't heard of the drop-in centre. It's very different from the Jobclub because it is so much more relaxed and a lot of people use it.

One reason why some focus group participants may have felt that Jobclub participation was mandatory was that ES advisers in some areas had used the Jobseeker's Direction to refer claimants to Jobclub. This focus group participant was a regular attendee at an employment access centre yet claimed that he had been "advised" to visit an official Jobclub and was resentful at what he clearly felt was pointless coercion:

If everyone refused to go to the Jobclubs, there wouldn't be any Jobclubs would there? So they've got to have some threat to make you go to them so they can stop your money. It's a lot of stress. To keep them sweet you just go even if you just sit there and drink tea for five hours a day, four days a week. Unless you've got a pea for a brain, you just go. It doesn't get you anywhere, but the worst thing you can do is say "I am not doing this" because they'll stop your money. To me, it's a game.

Work Trials

The Work Trials scheme enables an unemployed claimant to work for a potential employer who is looking to fill a vacancy on a trial basis for up to three weeks. During the period of the Work Trial claimants continue to receive their JSA plus travel and meal expenses. Under normal circum-stances a claimant must have been unemployed for at least six months prior to the start of the Work Trial period. If for any reason the Work Trial is not successful, the claimant continues to claim JSA and there are no benefit penalties. The rationale behind the Work Trials scheme is to offer Jobseekers the chance to try out different jobs and also demonstrate to an employer that they are suitable for the vacancy.

Focus group participant's opinions about the scheme were generally cynical. Although some felt that it might be useful for some people in certain circumstances, most of them were more reso-lute about their own employment capabilities and requirements. Many also felt that employers would exploit the scheme to obtain "cheap labour".

By contrast most key workers thought that Work Trials were valuable and particularly so for the long-term unemployed. The main problem for key workers was in trying to convince claimants of the scheme's potential value:

> I would say Work Trials' a good thing. .. They can prove that they can do the job. They're not going to lose out on their benefit if they decide that they don't want to take up the job. To sell Work Trial to the clients that sign on, it's an absolute nightmare. They don't want to know. All they see in it is the employer gets work out of you for three weeks and doesn't have to pay wages, and they're sort of blinkered you know.

Another problem reported by some key workers was that some clients were reluctant to present themselves to prospective employers in a manner which they perceived devalued them as pro-spective employees. A support worker in an employment access centre who had managed to convince a number of her clients go on Work Trials explained how some of her clients felt that the mechanics of operating the scheme took away their dignity:

> If somebody is really keen to do the job and they've been out of work for a long time, or they haven't got a lot of work experience, we explain what the Work Trials scheme is about and if they're happy to do it we advise them to put a Work Trial card in with the job application. But, they don't want to do that. What they want to do is get the job on their own merits first, and then offer to do it on a Work Trial basis. Some of them are a bit nervous, some of them just need a bit of space to get up to speed, to get that confidence back. We've had a lot of long term unemployed people get jobs and then only be able to hold them down for three or four weeks before being laid off...and I'm sure that's because they needed that time to adjust. I think employers are more willing to take a risk with somebody on a Work Trial.

With regard to the potential for exploitation by employers this support worker went on to say that:

Welfare-to-work and the long term unemployed

Work Trials can work really well but they have to monitored very carefully. I've had people who have gone on Work Trials and been told at the end of the first week "yes you've got the job", I've had other people that have gone on Work Trials, I've talked to the employer, I've said, "look, why wasn't this person suitable for the job" and it's quite clear they're exploiting the system and they didn't have a vacancy, and that person's been ripped off.

Another problem with Work Trials mentioned by some providers was that most employers were largely ignorant about the various schemes that the ES operated. Providers felt that the ES could and should do a lot more in terms of marketing their own schemes because employers were not going to take the initiative in finding out how they might be able recruit somebody who has been unemployed for over two years.

In terms of marketing Work Trials to claimants an ES frontline worker said that:

The sad thing about Work Trials is that basically the reason behind it is gone. It's just become a pure target, which is horribly difficult to fill, because the idea behind it has gone. You know, "you've got to get someone on Work Trials". Whether it's suitable for someone is by the by you know. Its just "we've got to have a certain number of people on Work Trials".

Employment subsidies and Personal Marketing Cards

We found various schemes operating in different areas all of which offered a financial incentive to employers to recruit an unemployed person. The vast majority of focus group participants claimed to know nothing about these schemes with the exception of some members of an all-women group in one area. Without being prompted they said they had been given what they referred to as 'Personal Marketing Cards' by ES staff who had encouraged them to use the cards in conjunction with job application forms. These cards indicated that the person was eligible for a Workstart employment subsidy for up to six months. The women were not convinced. They were reluctant to use the cards for similar reasons to those given for not making use of Work Trials:

You get cards now that you hand to, hopefully, your new employer, and they'll get money for taking you on. This makes it feel, from my point of view, that as a person there's nothing I've got to offer so why should I be a part of a scheme like that? It's so patronising.

We're supposed to take these cards to interviews. Even when you're applying for a job, you put it down on the application form. If you got a job with a small employer in a small business well, when that money stops that employer probably won't be able to pay you and that's it. I just got handed it and found the whole thing just laughable. If I was seriously applying for a job I wouldn't send it off to somebody. It's like sticking a £50 note in with your application. It takes away your dignity.

We discussed the details of this scheme with our other focus groups because it is likely to be a feature of the New Deal subsidies available to the older unemployed. The idea had few attractions. Most thought it sent out the wrong signal about the capacities they had to offer. However, one woman said that if the scheme was available in her area she would use it "just to see if it made any difference."

Travel to Interview Scheme

Focus group participants were asked about the Travel to Interview Scheme (TIS) which assists unemployed people to attend job interviews beyond their home area. Few participants had made use of TIS because their jobsearch was generally restricted to the local area. Some participants felt that the costs of travelling to all interviews ought to be met by the ES, especially if the ES was referring them to jobs:

> I find it really rough that if it's a local interview, say four or five miles, and you do it by car, you can't get expenses for that and, as a long-term unemployed person I could do with some help there.

A few participants had used TIS but felt that the administration of the scheme was unnecessarily complex. One man who had used the scheme on several occasions objected to the way the ES had checked out his attendance at the interview. He felt that by contacting the employer to confirm attendance the ES had undermined his credibility and jeopardised his chance of getting the job:

> It's worth bringing up travel expenses. I know that the Jobcentre do travelling expenses but they do it prior to the interview. You've just got a little bit of your self-respect and you get some person from the Jobcentre, however well-meaning, "Hello, it's the Job Centre here" [to the prospective employer]. You can't even get to the interview without the whole of the unemployment facility on your .. I'd like to be able to go into the Jobcentre and say "Look I've got an interview tomorrow, there's the letter, don't ring them up", you know. "I'll bring you the receipts, don't follow it through and hold my hand". Just stay out of the way, I need that little bit of humanity, that room to move, that might just get me the job!

Back-to-Work Bonus and assistance with initial work expenses

The Back-to-Work Bonus (BTWB) is available to claimants who have been entitled to JSA for thirteen weeks or more. It allows claimants to accrue credits against part time earnings whilst claiming JSA. These credits are equivalent to a proportion of the benefits that are deducted from the weekly allowance because of part time earnings. The credits are paid to the claimant as a tax-free lump sum when they sign off JSA. None of the focus group participants had considered making use of the BTWB scheme and most said they knew nothing about it. Those who had heard of BTWB rejected it on similar grounds to those given for rejecting the notion of part time work -

what they wanted was "full time work paying a living wage". When the details of the BTWB were explained to one focus group one participant made the following comment:

Why keep us hungry? If I work I want the money now.

When key workers were asked about the BTWB many of them referred to individual schemes that were operating locally which offered claimants a one-off payment when they found work and signed off. These payments were usually in the order of £200 to £300 and some offered an additional payment towards the costs of training. It was acknowledged that these one-off payments could help with some of the initial costs involved in getting work but they were only part of the solution to the financial uncertainties that faced a long term unemployed person taking a job:

They've got a new one now where if you get a low pay job you get £200 as a one-off sum. But you might be working in that low-paid job for five years, like that £200 isn't going to make a difference.

"If" and "Might" those are the two magic words for me. You are better off staying where you are because there's just too many imponderables.

S ince the late 1980s adult training provision has been targeted at the long-term unemployed. Through the focus groups we wanted to get some idea about the extent to which long term unemployed people made use of training opportunities, whether they thought that training or re-training would help them to find employment, and whether the training they had access to was appropriate. We also wanted to find out if there were any issues around access to training and further education particularly in relation to the benefit rules regarding part time study.

Attitudes towards training

Our research indicates that the way in which long term unemployed people negotiate and make sense of training opportunities is far from straightforward. In general, the claimants in our focus groups had a positive view of training, but access to appropriate training was a complex issue. The majority of those we talked to had either completed training courses, were currently involved in training or were contemplating taking up training in the near future. There were also a number of people who expressed a desire to take up training courses but for various reasons were unable to do so. Focus group participants generally engaged proactively with training opportunities, that is to say they felt that participation in training had been on their own initiative, rather than something that had been imposed on them as a condition of receiving benefits.

However, a significant number of focus group participants were less positive about the nature of much of the training that appeared to be accessible to them and those that had completed training courses in the past were sceptical about the value of training. Much of the scepticism about training came from the fact that despite having successfully completed training courses and gaining qualifications, focus group participants were still unable to find work.

> These training courses are all very good but there's no guarantee of a job from them. They say there might be but they don't say there will be. It's very unlikely. I'd go on a training course tomorrow if I'd get a job at the end of it.

> The thing for me is that I've done the courses but so have all the others I know. So we've got this and we've got that but it means nothing because there are too many people with them.

Another reason for scepticism about the value of training was that despite having completed courses and gained qualifications employers wanted people with experience:

I've done training. I've done six months of computer training but the point is you can do the training but when you come to look for jobs you need experience.

If you get on a course, even if it's a good course, and you get a qualification, you still haven't got the work experience and then it's hard to get someone interested in you... Employers can pick and choose.

Although some participants were disillusioned about training a larger group were either currently undertaking some form of training or seriously considering doing so. In almost all cases those we talked to claimed that they had taken the initiative to train and it was not something that had been imposed upon them. There were a few examples however where focus group participants felt that pressure had been put on them to take up specific courses. One woman explained why she had resisted being forced into joining a Training for Work (TfW) programme following a Restart Course:

They brought in people from outside to get you on these training schemes and you had to work for 13 weeks and if you stay for 13 weeks, I found out later, then they got commission. But when I went back to my DEA [Disability Advisor] and I said they want me to do this thing she said "Well, do you want to do it?" And I said "No" and she said "Well, you don't have to then, they're on commission." But they were telling the people on Restart that if you didn't go then you'd lose all your benefits you know? They were actually threatening people do you know what I mean?

A provider of adult literacy and numeracy courses operating under the TfW scheme explained some of the difficulties she faced when prospective trainees felt pressurised to attend her courses:

One of the problems we have is that it is often perceived by the clients that they are being told to come here, and obviously as time goes on there will be more and more compulsion but at this moment TfW is voluntary but they can be under pressure. They can direct people to come here for an interview but I might say "no, this person isn't suitable". Or they might equally say "look, I really don't need this" in which case we have to find a form of words that is going to be acceptable so that they wont have their benefit docked. But we don't want people here who don't want to be here because it makes our job very unpleasant, if not almost impossible.

Access to training

While attitudes towards training were generally positive some of those we interviewed faced significant barriers, especially those who wanted to do higher level courses. Others criticised recent changes to TfW, which limited the availability of courses, and of eligibility rules which could deny them access.

Some people were clearly frustrated at not being able to access the level of training or education that they thought would help them even though in some cases they had explored a variety of avenues:

> I tried to get another course recently but there's only one provider in this whole area for the training (and) a couple of weeks ago I found out that I couldn't get on it. I'd like to go to the local university to do a degree in this area but I now realise that I've left it too late. It would be a real problem to live on so little money.

> It's just impossible to get the training you want. The trouble is that you can get into a degree course but you get £1,710 a year and you can't live on it with a mortgage and everything and you have only that for three or four years.

> I did a full-time course in general clerical work doing NVQs at Level 2. One and half days a week, and I was led to believe that I could go on, in theory, up to Level 5. I got this [Level 2] in April 1994 and I have been totally unable to progress onto any course that would lead to NVQ Level 3, totally impossible, and it took me two and a half odd years to find out why. It's just the usual bullshit, they don't tell you. The main reason is that now Level 3 is a supervisory level and you have to be an employee to progress to Level 3 so I've just had bits and bobs. I just feel that the ES is very unhelpful. You ask questions but you just get fobbed off or misinformed and you waste a lot of time.

One training provider argued that for many of the long term unemployed people she came into contact with TfW was not appropriate because it was limited to NVQ Levels 1 and 2. She also highlighted similar problems to those referred to above:

> Something like a quarter of the people that are around here actually need to retrain. There's no TfW provision for them because .. we're talking about people that need to do NVQ 4. And it's just not available. Or, they need specialised courses which they can only do as an HNC or a higher level course. Now they know that if they do those courses they can get jobs at the end but it's the financing. Just lately we've had three or four people through who are looking at the issue of going on to do a (Diploma in Social Work). But the grant situation is such that they're not sure if they can afford to do it with their financial commitments and mortgages etc. So what they're saying is "I've got to weigh this up, the short term against the long term you know? And that is something that's coming up more and more often, particularly with people over 25.

Some people made a sharp distinction between voluntary training courses and Government training schemes:

> *I went on a business scheme. I got to it through the Job Centre but it wasn't compulsory. It was about starting your own business and that sort of thing. It was fantastic, 100% really professional. I was really nervous but she sat me down and explained everything perfectly and by the time I left there I knew exactly what I was doing. So if you wanted to go into self-employment, it was great. It was excellent but I think that was funded by the European Union. I don't know anyone that has benefited from any of the other schemes, this Job Training crap.*

By contrast some focus group participants could not understand why there were barriers to joining the TfW scheme:

> *These courses should be open to everybody rather than wait until you've been unemployed for six months or whatever. Then people who have not been unemployed for long but want to get into work can do it. The rigidity of the programmes is so stupid.*

Others were similarly aggrieved about the eligibility rules and had experienced problems about getting onto courses. A lot of the comments about training schemes were inter-mingled with comments about "fiddling the figures". This was highlighted during one conversation where one person was explaining how he had wanted to take up a TfW place but was prevented from doing so by the eligibility rules:

> *I was on a course for a couple of months which took me out of the system. I was still on benefits but they didn't require me to sign on for a couple of months therefore I wasn't officially signed on to JSA. That's one of the reasons why I cannot go for a Training For Work course because I have not been six months unemployed but in fact I've been unemployed for four years.*

> *I'd been on a course for about six months and when I went back [to sign on at the Jobcentre] I'm now unemployed from the date I went back not from the date when I was originally made redundant, which was in 1989!*

> *Yeah, I don't know what happened to me. On the computer it said that I was seven months unemployed but in fact I've been unemployed for about five years!*

Part time study: The 16 Hour Rule

Many of those we talked to had some knowledge of the JSA part time study rules, and some demonstrated a good working knowledge of the regulations. Some of them also suggested that ES staff exercised discretion when applying these rules:

You can get courses where you're doing two and a half days a week but it depends on who your counsellor is when you go to sign on [if you encounter problems with enforcement of the 16 hour rule]. Some of my friends are doing two and a half days a week courses for an NVQ, but it all depends.

I was going to do an NVQ once and they [Jobcentre staff] said that was OK. I think that they have a lot of room for manoeuvre, they treat people how they want to.

Some people had experienced problems doing courses on a part time basis when the ES enforced rules about attending review interviews. Some focus group participants clearly felt that the ES had tried to make life difficult for them:

They [Jobcentre staff] can actually cause you problems. You can be doing things which are outside of what they're going to tick you off as doing. For example, I went on a training course. I'd been there for about three months and I went into the Jobcentre right, and I had a Restart interview with a woman down at the Jobcentre and it ended up, after a little bit of argy-bargy backwards and for-wards, as she said at the end, "Oh, of course, you've got to this and this and this" and I said that I was down at (course provider) and she said "I can take you off that tomorrow." .. It's European-funded and so she's not going to get the little tick on the paper. And it was very good training but she threatened to actually take me off the course though she didn't actually do it.

One focus group participant felt that ES priorities were at odds with providing genuine help for unemployed claimants:

The trouble with JSA and everything else is that it seems that the Employment Offices are working against training. For instance we're only allowed to do fif-teen hours a week. Now that seems stupid because if you're unemployed and you want to get a job it should be the case that you should be allowed to do seven days a week if you want to get somewhere. So that's the first restriction. And the other thing is the actual attitude. .. It's a case that any sort of job is more important than any sort of training! There's no priority put on training! It's just get a job and get off the record.

All the training providers we spoke to who ran non-TfW training courses reported problems with the ES. The incidence and frequency of these occurrences varied widely between and within different Jobcentres. Training providers cited three main types of problem: ES staff inappropri-ately applying the 16 hour rule to ESF funded courses; ES staff insisting that claimants attend Restart Courses or Jobplan Workshops mid way through other courses; and, ES staff threatening to take Jobseekers off of courses. Training providers felt that many of these problems resulted from ignorance of the complex rules on the part of ES staff that was often exacerbated by inexperience resulting from staff turnover. One training and education manager providing courses funded by the ESF explained some of the problems he had encountered:

> There's a big difference from Jobcentre to Jobcentre. There's also a difference between Client Advisers. When you get staff turnover they start doing silly things like: "16 hours, that's it, no exceptions" which of course is not the case for ESF funded courses. .. We recently had one student who had been signing on, he came to do this course, he went in and told the Jobcentre and they promptly stopped his benefits. I got on the phone and spoke to a Client Adviser. What had actually happened was he went in went up to the reception desk the clerical staff on the reception desk said "over 16 hours", ticked the box on the form, stopped his benefits. It never even went as far as the Client Adviser to determine eligibility. ... When I phoned up I eventually spoke to a Benefits Manager and as far as she was concerned, anything over 16 hours, I don't pay. Speaking to the Benefits Manager I actually quoted the Jobseeker's Regulations, Ministerial statements, referred her to Hansard, referred her to the Adjudication Guide, the reply was, she did not understand all the terminology, her guidelines are 16 hours. .. What it's meant is that I've had to spend a large amount of time on the telephone training Client Advisers how to run their own regulations. .. I started cataloguing these problems in October 1996. I'll quite often make four phone calls a day sorting this stuff out. .. The problem is that when they're threatened with losing their benefits they leave the course and that it is what we're trying to stop.

Another training provider in another area who also ran ESF funded training courses felt that some ES staff created unnecessary bureaucratic barriers:

> I've had to write letters (to the ESJ) for nearly everybody saying it's only 15 hours per week, stating the times and places and that we supply all the materials. And I've had two letters from the TEC to back me up...So we've limited the hours to 15 to safeguard their benefits. But the ES keep phoning up trying to find out anything that will trip them up.

Another training provider felt that although the regulations caused her staff some problems, the impact on trainees was minimal because they had grown accustomed to complying with the dictates of the JSA regulations:

> We try and keep up to date with all of that and it is very important because we've got to watch how many hours people are here as opposed to how many hours they should be here to achieve anything. We've got to encourage them to do everything by the board and as things get narrowed down so we find ourselves having to do a lot more work on the telephone to the ES and the DSS and places like that. People come up here, and certainly because of the changes,

have been having to attend other things rather than us, then they're allowed to come over here but also, people are very acquiescent about this. They don't actually moan and groan about it because they feel that if they do, they'll lose their benefits.

The issues around Further Education were similar to those regarding training with access sometimes hampered by ES staff inflexibly applying the part-time study rules. Advice agency intervention usually sorted out these problems and claimants tended to experience fewer problems with the 16-hour rule if they went to advice agencies before telling the ES about the course. An Advice and Guidance Officer at one FE College explained how:

some students go down to the Jobcentre and say that they want to do a course and say all the wrong things before they've spoken to us...and we say "oh no, you didn't say that did you!"

However, some focus group participants who had considered taking FE courses resented having to study on a part-time basis because it would take longer to complete the course which in turn means longer on the unemployment register:

It seems daft to me. If I want to go to college I can only be part-time, which means I'm on the register for longer, which means I'm costing the tax-payer even more! It's crazy

Welfare-to-work and the long term unemployed

6. Evaluating labour market programmes and users' opinions

All political parties now agree that active labour market programmes are playing an essential part in modernising the welfare state. However, there continue to be acute controversies about the particular mix of programmes and about their relative effectiveness.

This part of the report assesses evidence about the impact of some of the key British programmes which have been aimed at helping the long term unemployed back into work. It draws on both published and unpublished evaluation evidence and, for the reasons outlined in the introduction, the focus is on those ES delivered programmes that are most likely to have been experienced by the older long term unemployed and are of most relevance to the programmes now being delivered by the new Government.

Although programmes are usually evaluated against their individual objectives this report concentrates on two broad types of assistance. The next chapter considers job search assistance and looks at the impact of Jobclubs; Restart and caseloading interviews; short courses, including compulsory ones such as Jobplan Workshops; and the Travel to Interview scheme. The subsequent chapter assesses different types of work experience programmes, including temporary work programmes; Workstart employment subsidies; and Work Trials.

The report reviews much of the quantitative evidence available on the outcomes of participants but we supplement this wherever we can with qualitative evidence from interviews with participants. We also try to place this evidence in the institutional and historical contexts in which individual programmes operated.

Evaluation concepts

There is no single measure of effectiveness and this report makes no attempt to resolve the many complex issues and debates about how to assess the impact of labour market programmes. However, before it is possible to draw on the evidence from evaluation studies it is important to describe some of the key measures that are used to evaluate schemes.

The first, the **job entry rate** refers to the proportion of programme participants who leave the programme for a job or who get a job shortly after leaving. This is the most common way in which British programmes have been evaluated, and regular surveys are conducted to establish the destinations of those leaving a wide variety of programmes. The job entry rate is a crude measure of the effectiveness of programmes because it does not take into account what would have happened to participants had they not participated. It can also be misleading if the recruitment to and eligibility for individual programmes result in selection bias. For example, it is relatively easy to achieve a high job entry rate with a programme targeted on those who employers would choose more easily, for example those who possess relatively high skills, confidence and motivation.

The proportion of people getting work through a programme who would have done so without the assistance is called deadweight. Once **deadweight** has been subtracted from job entry rates we get a measure of what some would describe as the real effect of the programme on unemployed individual's employment prospects **(job entry net of deadweight)**. Unfortunately this measure is hard to assess for both practical and methodological reasons and is rarely estimated for British programmes.

Comparing programmes

There have been a number of attempts to use existing evaluation data to compare programmes with one another in terms of cost effectiveness. For example, in a recent report for the Joseph Rowntree Foundation, Gardiner undertakes an analysis of the "annual unit cost per additional person in work" for a number of programmes (1997, p. 32). According to Gardiner, these figures tell us "how much it costs under each scheme to get someone into a job who would not have found work otherwise". Each figure is derived by dividing the unit cost of the programme by an estimate of the job entry rate net of deadweight for the scheme.

Gardiner makes this calculation for all those schemes for which evidence was collected and then draws conclusions about relative cost effectiveness. Her conclusion is that "Jobfinder's Grant and Jobmatch perform best according to relative measures of effectiveness" (ibid, p. 42). Unfortunately, Gardiner's report is an example of the misleading results that can arise from trying to make comparisons that are not supported by the available data. Put simply, Gardiner is not comparing like with like. Deadweight for the programmes she concludes were most effective was in fact estimated on a totally different basis from most of the other programmes she compares them with. In fact, most of the deadweight estimates come from studies using control groups, but the estimates for Jobfinder's Grant and Jobmatch were precisely those that had been evaluated differently with deadweight estimated through calculations based on those participants who said that they would have got into work without the programmes; a technique which is likely to give very different results from a control group study.

This report makes no attempt to use the evaluation evidence to make direct comparisons between *different* types of programmes, for a number of good reasons.

Firstly, programmes have, by necessity, been evaluated using different methods and at different times. Each method has different problems and sources of error and will therefore give different results, as will evaluations undertaken at different stages in the economic cycle. This means it is highly unlikely that existing British data can be used to make meaningful comparisons between programmes.

Even where comparisons can be made on the basis of outcomes net of deadweight, the picture is complicated by substitution and displacement effects. As a result, there is no single measure that can be used to assess effectiveness. If one is interested in preventing inflation, for example, then training programmes to reduce skill shortages might be considered most effective. If one is more concerned to redistribute jobs to the unemployed in an attempt to reduce the number of workless households, then programmes with higher substitution and displacement effects may be appropriate.

Effectiveness also varies from one participant to the next. One of the most important findings of a recent evaluation study of several job search assistance programmes (White et al, 1997) is that some programmes assist certain groups into work but have no impact (or even a negative impact) on the employment prospects of other groups. For example, Jobclub was found to increase the chances of entering employment by nearly 30% for men without vocational qualifications, but for men with vocational qualifications Jobclub was found to actually **reduce** the chances of entering employment by 12%. Other evidence suggests that it is **combinations** of different types of intervention which are most effective. This suggests that there is a need for a range of programmes for unemployed people, and that some options will be more appropriate for some people than others.

Users opinions

As well as studying the outcomes achieved by programmes we can learn a lot by analysing the opinions of those who have had first hand experience of employment and training programmes, including unemployed participants, staff and employers. Most government evaluations include a qualitative study of users' opinions about the programme. There are also general surveys of unemployed people that give insights into how programmes actually operate on the ground, which elements of programmes are most effective and which need improving, and what kinds of people each programme works for. They can also provide an historical and institutional context within which to interpret outcome data.

One key source of claimants' opinions of the whole range of government programmes has been the ES National Customer Satisfaction Survey. In the 1993 survey claimants who had pursued programmes as a result of attendance at a Restart interview were asked whether the decision to pursue the programme was taken by them or by their adviser. The authors concluded that "there was a definite thrust for vocational, work related programmes coming from claimants themselves

They're very cynical

... Conversely, ES staff were more instrumental in the attendance of job search skills programmes" (Smith and Stallwood, 1994, p. 80-81).

The 1994 survey (the last one which asked these questions) found that claimants who had attended programmes on average seemed to regard them as being fairly good. There was no clear discernible pattern as to the type of programmes which were considered best, except for strong support for Learning for Work, a pilot programme which allowed claimants access to full time education (Nove and Smith, 1995, p. 113).

On the other hand, when the same people were asked what effect they thought the programme had had on their job prospects, in general they tended "not to feel that the schemes [had] made a great deal of difference" (ibid, p. 115). This may be partly an inevitable result of interviewing claimants: the very fact that they are still unemployed suggests that the programme hasn't worked for them. The same survey interviewed a small group of non-claimants who had attended programmes and they were somewhat more positive, with just over half believing the programme had improved their job prospects.

It is important to remember that taking the average opinion also fails to capture the important differences between individual experiences. Every programme will help some people more than others, and the opinions participants express clearly reflect this. For example, the Restart Course is one of the least popular programmes, and in a postal survey 20% of respondents said it was not very useful and 12% said it was not at all useful. Nevertheless, 21% of people found the same programme very useful (Public Attitude Surveys Ltd, 1996, p. 17). This may reflect different standards of course delivery, but it also shows the need for a range of assistance to suit individual needs.

This section covers programmes, which aim to increase the effectiveness of unem ployed people's job search. There are three broad categories of assistance: short courses teaching job search skills; intensive caseloading interviews with ES staff to discuss, improve and police job search activity; and provision of resources to improve individuals' job search.

Job Search courses

Short courses providing group training in job search activities have been available to unemployed people since Restart Courses were introduced in 1986. Job search courses aim "to give people the knowledge, skills and motivation to mount and carry through an effective jobsearch campaign" (Employment Service, 1994, intro, p. 2) and they also function as a recruitment route for other employment and training programmes. They include activities such as identifying and pursuing vacancies, completion of application forms, drafting and updating CVs, and coaching in interview techniques. Although the ES has usually been able to offer non-mandatory courses to some of the shorter term unemployed most of this provision has been compulsory, and aimed at the long term unemployed.

In 1990, Restart Courses became mandatory for all claimants unemployed for two years who refused offers of a place on a government scheme at their 24-month advisory (Restart) interview. The number of people required to attend compulsory job search courses then increased dramatically, especially after compulsory Jobplan Workshops were extended to those out of work for over a year. By 1994/95 248,400 people were required to attend Jobplan, and another 147,100 attended Restart Courses (DfEE, 1997, Tables 8.12 and 8.13). Subsequently, the number of places on compulsory job search courses declined because the emphasis shifted to compulsory caseloading interview programmes (see below).

The impact of job search courses

Evidence on the effectiveness of job search courses is rather mixed. The gross job entry rates recorded in management information for the courses are very low. For example, only around four per cent of participants on the largest compulsory programme, Jobplan Workshop, get a job as a direct result of participation. (Murray, 1996, p. 17 & 20).

They're very cynical

However, more effective control group studies have been conducted on Jobplan Workshop and Workwise courses for the under 25s.

The Jobplan study used a randomised trial (see Appendix B) and found that 24% of those referred to Jobplan had left the unemployment register 16 weeks later compared to 19% of the control group. This suggested that 5% of those referred had left the register due to a 'Jobplan effect' (Kay, 1994). However, there is no firm evidence that this register effect reflected people going into jobs. Only 2.1% more people went into jobs from the programme group; a result that was not statistically significant.

An analysis of register 'off-flows' was also undertaken. This examined changes in the patterns of people leaving the unemployment register before and after the introduction of Jobplan (Birtwhistle and Looby, 1994). The study found that there was a "clear and significant increase in the rate of off-flows from the unemployment register of those unemployed between 58 and 78 weeks" (ibid, 2.1) between 1992 and 1993. However, this study used data that did not include information about where people went when they signed off so once again it cannot be concluded that in-creased register off-flows translated into people getting jobs.

It is also unclear that the increase in off-flows occurred as a result of Jobplan. Jobplan was intro-duced in April 1993, but the study found that by the first quarter of 1993 off flows had already increased compared with the same period in 1992, despite the absence of Jobplan (ibid, Annex 1). This suggests that the increase in off-flows may have been due to other factors "such as increasing ES effectiveness with this client group" (ibid, 4.15). This is quite likely because "we know that the total number of Restart interviews conducted in 1993/94 (3.3 million) was half a million more than in the previous year and that the numbers referred to Government schemes directly as a result of these interventions increased from 400,000 in 1992/93 to 730,000 in 1993/94" (Murray, 1996, p. 21).

A subsequent study of the initial pilot four week Workwise courses used a control group from the areas not involved. The results were disappointing. Those referred to Workwise actually secured worse outcomes than those who had been referred to Jobplan. The differences were small: 18% of those referred to Workwise were in work or training five months later, compared to 22% referred to Jobplan. The difference was not found to be statistically significant so it was concluded that "there is no difference in effectiveness between Workwise and Jobplan" (Kay et al, 1995, p. 3).

Between April 1995 and 1997, Workwise was operated as part of a package with 1-2-1, a pro-gramme of caseloading interviews (discussed later). This is the only programme that has been found by a control group study to have a significant effect on job outcomes. The evaluation (Kay and Fletcher, 1996) compared a randomly selected programme group that was referred to 1-2-1/Workwise with a control group that was offered no provision. After 24 weeks, 14.3% of those referred to the programme were in work compared with 9.5% of the control group.

Welfare-to-work and the long term unemployed

These studies suggest that job search courses may have at best a small effect in terms of getting people into work, but they do often increase the numbers leaving the register. So what happens to those people who leave the register but do not get jobs?

The Jobplan evaluation found that half of them started a government training scheme and half were no longer signing "for reasons not reported to the ES" (Kay, 1994, p. 8). The 1-2-1/Workwise evaluation found that referral to the programme increased the proportion entering TfW from 4.4% to 8.6% and the proportion simply failing to sign from 4.4% to 6.5% (24 weeks later).

Other evidence suggests that these two outcomes are important effects of job search courses. According to management information, while around a third of participants on Jobplan Work-shop and Workwise achieve some form of 'positive outcome', between a half and three quarters of these outcomes simply involve the individual starting on another government scheme (Murray, 1996). It is useful to note that many of these outcomes will not be picked up in the evaluation studies because the studies only measure those leaving the register whereas participants on many programmes (e.g. Jobclub, Job Interview Guarantee) continue to sign on.

There is also some evidence to suggest that being referred to a compulsory job search course encourages claimants to drop off the register. Over half of those referred to Workwise or Jobplan fail to start on the programme (ibid). Clearly some of these people will have got jobs before the programme starts but others may simply have signed off, some of whom may have been claiming fraudulently, or claimed sickness benefits (a factor confirmed in our focus group findings).

Another significant factor which has undermined the credibility of the courses and of the man-agement information collected has been referred to as 'target chasing', where returns to the ES from course providers are manipulated in order to secure future contracts and satisfy ES targets (Blagg et al, 1994, p. 17). This seemed to be confirmed by a postal survey of Jobplan participants, which found "significant discrepancies between the recorded management information and the referrals claimed by respondents", especially those relating to job referrals (DVL Smith, 1994, p. 16). It was discovered that a mere "12% of those recorded in the management information as being referred to a job/job interview claimed to have been referred".

Blagg et al also found that some course leaders "have felt under pressure to distort their advice to clients to satisfy ES regional office requests to meet targets for Jobclubs, Community Action and so on" (1994, p. 17). Wright & Cooper argued that "provider target chasing at the expense of realistic longer term outcomes was evident" among Workwise providers. They found that "some providers sought ES "brownie points" from high outcomes, and employed a mixture of misinfor-mation, cajoling and pressure to achieve dubious client commitment to action plans" (1996, p. 47).

They're very cynical

Participants' views on job search courses: the impact of compulsion

Participants themselves have widely differing views about job search courses. In general, claimants seem to prefer training and work experience programmes but on the other hand some people found the courses very helpful.

Most of the negative views expressed reflect poor targeting. Jobsearch courses were targeted at unemployed people who had reached certain durations of unemployment, at which point they were required to attend unless they take up another option such as a place on a programme. This form of targeting has a number of negative consequences. Restricting access to people unemployed for over a year is frustrating for some shorter-term unemployed claimants who feel they would benefit from a course (see NACAB, 1994, p. 27). It is also likely that job search courses are most useful early in a period of unemployment, because they have been found to be most suitable for people who do not have a clear idea of what kind of job they want. Indeed, over a quarter of participants on Job Review Workshop (a voluntary programme available after three months unemployment) felt the course had been offered too late while only 5% felt it had been offered too early (Heather & Kay, 1995, p. 36).

On the other hand, a lot of people for whom a job search course is unsuitable, or not the best form of help, are forced to participate after a year or two years of unemployment. This undoubtedly reduces the effectiveness of the course. A comparison of participant attitudes to Jobplan Workshop (compulsory at a year or 18 months unemployment) and Job Search Seminars (another voluntary course that was available after three months unemployment) illustrates this effect (see table 2).

Table 1: Participant opinions of Jobplan and Job Search Seminars

How helpful/useful was the programme?	Jobplan Workshop (compulsory)	Job Search Seminar (voluntary)
Very	15%	33%
Quite/Fairly	49%	53%
Not very	24%	11%
Not at all	11%	3%

Source: DVL Smith Ltd (1994, p. 33) [excluding no answer/don't knows]; Duxbury & Ward (1993, p. 22).

Welfare-to-work and the long term unemployed

Similarly, 14% of Jobplan participants found the course worse than they had expected compared with only 6% of participants on the voluntary Job Review Workshop, despite prior expectations of Jobplan already being low (DVL Smith Ltd, 1994, p. 37; Heather & Kay, 1995, p. 36).

Job search courses work for some people but not for others. For example, on leaving Jobplan, 34% of participants stated that they felt more confident and optimistic about getting a job than before, but 60% "reported that Jobplan had made no difference to their attitude in terms of optimism and confidence". A further 6% left Jobplan actually feeling less optimistic (DVL Smith Ltd, 1994, p. 37).

Another study of Jobplan concluded that "perceived benefits varied enormously within work-shops as a result of individual differences in client needs" (Blagg et al, 1994, emphasis added).

Because these differences in needs are not taken into account, compulsion is strongly resisted by many clients, as illustrated both in the findings of our focus groups and by the high numbers of people who have their benefit cut for non-attendance or early leaving. In 1995/96 for example, 364,900 people started a compulsory job search programme and 79,000 people were sanctioned for failing to attend or complete the scheme (Murray, 1996a, table 3).

A postal survey of Jobplan participants found "a core of around 25% to 30% of respondents who seem fundamentally negatively disposed towards the scheme" (DVL Smith Ltd, 1994, p. (ii)). Furthermore, they found very strong condemnation of the programme from between 5% and 10% of the sample, indeed 5% went as far as to comment unprompted that Jobplan should be abandoned (ibid, p. 46-7).

It has been suggested that compulsory courses function as a means of "identifying benefit abuse", but the problem is that such courses are a very blunt instrument for doing so. Unwilling recruits make for difficult sessions and other people undertaking legitimate activities within the benefit regulations to improve their employability, such as voluntary work or part-time study are often reluctant to attend (Donnelly, 1997, p. 14; NACAB, 1994, p. 19).

The presence of unwilling participants causes problems for the course providers. Blagg et al found that some clients, for example those with "severe domestic and personal problems" were "likely to refuse to participate" which was "very disruptive to the rest of the workshop" (1994, p. 12). Some of the comments of workshop leaders suggest a constant struggle to keep participants co-operative and a tendency to be flexible about attendance in order to get people to turn up at all (Wright & Cooper, 1996, p. 46). Compulsory courses are also very hard to 'sell' to claimants, who fairly naturally assume that because they are being forced to attend it is not something they would want to go on.

They're very cynical

Who benefits from jobsearch courses?

Studies are remarkably consistent on the question of whom job search courses are and are not suitable for. In general it seems that job search courses are suited to "younger clients with a less well defined occupational direction, or, alternatively, with transferable skills such as sales or cleri-cal/secretarial competence" (DVL Smith Ltd, 1994, p. 40).

Older people tend to make negative comments about the atmosphere and generally get less from courses (ibid). This is likely to be because they have a better idea of what they want to do and all the studies conclude that job search courses are not suitable for people who have clear employ-ment goals and/or know what they are going to do to achieve them (ibid, p. 42; Blagg et al, 1994, p. 20; Wright & Cooper, 1996, p. 5-6).

Other people for whom courses seem less suitable include (Blagg et al, 1994; Wright & Cooper, 1996):

● those with "severe domestic problems, health problems, psychological difficulties, or social problems (homelessness alcoholism, criminal record)";

● claimants in the benefit trap due, for example, to high housing costs;

● people who are involved in voluntary work or part-time study who usually "honestly believe that their new qualifications will increase their employability" (Wright & Cooper, 1996, p. 29);

● those in rural areas who have long, difficult journeys to the course; and

● people who have been on a course before.

Forcing people who have been on a course before to attend again or attend a different yet similar course is highly counter-productive and elicits strong feelings from participants who frequently complain that a course offers them "nothing new" (DVL Smith Ltd 1994, p. 43). One study, considering job search training within TfW found that "the group approach to job search training was often both ineffective and unpopular with the trainees, many of whom had been through the system before" (Quality Assurance Division, 1994).

For this reason it may be highly significant that the control group studies considered above have all been conducted near the start of a programme's life, and where they have not, only first referrals to the programme have been included in the analysis (Kay et al, 1995, p. 5). As the number of places on compulsory job search programmes has increased, more and more people will have been referred for a second or third time, which is likely to have reduced the effectiveness of the programmes and increased the negative experiences of participants.

Good practice guidelines

Despite the concerns about compulsion, motivation and target chasing, there is clear evidence that some elements of job search training can be usefully delivered in groups. Participants who like the courses comment in particular on the usefulness of CV preparation, learning interview and phone techniques and how to complete application forms (DVL Smith Ltd, 1994, p. 43; Wright & Cooper, 1996, p. 23). They also like having a chance to meet other people in a "similar situation". It also seems that participants who move from a job search course into another programme are significantly more likely to find the course useful than those who simply keep signing on (DVL Smith Ltd, 1994, p. 35).

Studies based on the opinions of participants suggest a number of guidelines for good practice in delivering job search courses:

- groups should be small or courses won't work (Blagg et al, 1994, p. 25);

- courses cannot cater for too diverse a range of participants. All of the studies emphasise the need for courses targeted at "homogeneous groups (skill/ability/age/work/experience)" (DVL Smith Ltd, 1994, p. 53). Some participants did like Workwise because it involved only young unemployed people (Wright & Cooper, 1996, p. 23-4). Managerial and professional people were "markedly less positive about Jobplan than other groups", and many felt it was "not really 'for them'" (DVL Smith Ltd, 1994, p. 39 & 53);

- staff should not be patronising. Clients complained about a classroom atmosphere or about impersonal staff with a lack of empathy (ibid, p. 43/52; Blagg et al, 1994, p. 13 & 18);

- staff should be properly trained and experienced. This is difficult under existing contractual arrangements. Wright & Cooper found that "few Workwise Leaders had attended specialist Workwise training courses, and over 50% were on short term (hourly) contracts" (1996, p. 6);

- there should be sufficient resources and leaders to ensure that participants do not find themselves sitting around with nothing to do for much of the time, a problem complained of by some participants (DVL Smith Ltd, 1994, p. 50; Blagg et al, 1994, p. 8); and

- there is a need for much better communication between Jobcentres and course providers. Not only does it seem that there is a lack of face to face contact between ES staff and course leaders (Wright & Cooper, 1996, p. 19), but there was evidence of considerable mistrust between the two groups. For example, Workwise leaders talked of ES advisers "passing on their problems" to courses (ibid, p. 16). Jobplan leaders generally resisted quality monitoring by ES staff and took the view that "ES staff ... were not in a position to judge the quality of the Jobplan workshops" (Blagg et al, 1994, p. 24).

Restart and Caseloading Interviews

Since the creation of the ES unemployed people have always been able, or required, to attend interviews with Jobcentre staff in order to discuss aspects of their claim or possibilities of work or training, and there have also been specialist staff who could work with individuals on a more structured basis. However, from the mid-1980s regular compulsory interviews became more common and by the early 1990s compulsory attendance at a structured series of interviews began to be extended to cover the longer-term unemployed.

In 1986 compulsory Restart interviews (as distinct from Restart courses) were piloted and in 1987/88 they were extended to create a national system of six monthly interviews for all unemployed claimants. At these interviews (which are still part of the present system) advisers review claimants' job seeking activities and offer clients a menu of options to pursue such as jobs, training or other programmes. Where suitable, they also suggest to claimants that they should consider claiming another benefit, such as a disability or carers benefit.

The Restart programme was considered to be highly successful and in 1994 compulsory interviews were extended with the introduction of two new programmes called 1-2-1 (aimed at 18 to 25 year olds unemployed for over a year and linked with Workwise) and Jobfinder (aimed at those out of work over two years).

Each programme comprises a series of six or seven (usually fortnightly) structured interviews with a single ES adviser, a process that is referred to as 'intensive caseloading'. Advisers should help claimants by "giving counselling in job search techniques and helping clients to devise a realistic route into work or appropriate training." (Lourie, 1997, p. 43). Claimants are required to attend 1-2-1 after twelve months unemployment and Jobfinder after two years unemployment if they refuse to take up another offer at a Restart interview. Refusal or failure to attend is likely to lead to a cut in benefit.

The numbers attending Restart interviews and caseloading interviews ebbs and flows with the overall unemployment total with, for example, the number attending Restart interviews falling from a high point of 3.7m in 1994/95 to just over 3.2m in 1996/97. However, over the period the number of long term unemployed people being required to attend linked caseloading interviews increased noticeably. In 1996/97 218,241 people out of work for over a year attended 1-2-1, and in 1997/98 190,000 of those out of work for over two years were expected to participate in Jobfinder . The new Government will build on this approach and from June 1998 a new 'Jobfinder Plus' programme is to be aimed at unemployed people aged over 25, primarily those crossing the 18 month threshold of unemployment. It will consist of a "series of one to one interviews with a dedicated adviser to identify the best means of helping them move into sustainable employment" (DfEE, 1998, p. 105).

The impact of Restart Interviews

The most influential study of Restart interviews was published in 1992 (White & Lakey, 1992). It was used by the then Employment Secretary to justify the expansion of Restart as the results "clearly" demonstrated "the effectiveness of the Restart programme in getting people back into work" (Finn, 1993).

The researchers conducted a randomised control group study to analyse the effect of Restart interviews on claimants who were six months unemployed. They found that those referred to an interview on average spent around 5% less time in claimant unemployment over the following year than those in the control group. They also left unemployment sooner, and were less likely to spend the whole of the next year unemployed.

As we know, however, more people leaving the register does not always translate into more people in jobs or other positive outcomes. There was strong evidence that Restart increased the time clients spent on training schemes and other government programmes and reduced the time they took to enter such programmes. The evidence on job entry, however, was considerably weaker. People referred to Restart did on average enter work more quickly than the control group, but they did not spend a significantly greater total amount of time in work over the following year (White & Lakey, 1992, p. 115).

This is an example of how using a broader outcome indicator (in this case the total amount of time spent in work over the subsequent year) can give a very different picture of the effectiveness of a programme. The authors attributed the failure of Restart to have a significant effect on this indicator to the fact that most of the jobs available at the time for long term unemployed people were short-term or insecure. Although they found "no evidence that Restart itself fosters short-lived jobs", the prevalence of short-term jobs generally (among the jobs available to the unemployed) "places a constraint on what can be achieved by a service like Restart" (ibid, 116).

It is likely that any longer term effect of Restart on participant's job prospects could only be achieved by programmes and services to which people are referred from Restart, as the authors of the study point out:

> Restart's potential depends partly upon the other programmes and services to which it is linked. If these are not geared to raising aspects of job quality, then it is unlikely that Restart will do so (White & Lakey, 1992, p. 168-9).

Indeed, it could be suggested that the main effect of Restart has been to provide a gateway to other programmes and services. The most significant effect of Restart was increased participation in programmes, and it may well be that the limited evidence of a 'Restart effect' on job outcomes can be accounted for by the effects of this participation. For example, White and Lakey found that those successfully placed into an option at Restart subsequently had better outcomes in terms of leaving the register than those who were submitted to an option but not successfully placed and those who refused the offer (1992, p. 78). These differences may be accounted for by differences in the characteristics of these different groups (because disadvantaged claimants were harder to place in an option) but it is impossible to know for sure because what happened to each client at Restart (i.e. whether placed in an option or not) is not included as an independent variable in the multivariate analyses used to demonstrate the Restart effect.

The other main effect of Restart was on 'sign-offs', the number of people leaving the register and entering a "non-claimant, non-employed" status (including claiming other benefits but excluding time on government programmes). The initial effect of Restart was to increase sign-offs:

> a clear Restart effect emerges within about one month of the date of the coun-
> selling interview. ... at this early stage movement into a non-claimant status is
> the main component of the Restart effect (White & Lakey, 1992, p. 166).

This led to an increase in the total amount of time in non-claimant status during the six months after the interview, but after six months people tended to sign on again, which meant that in total, across the entire twelve months following the interview, there was no significant effect on the amount of time spent in non-claimant status.

Although this suggests that people signing off come back again, it is worrying that the initial effect is there. An investigation of why people signed off found that most people did so for reasons connected with illness, disability or caring responsibilities. These can all be criteria for claiming other benefits. That Restart encouraged people to sign-off and claim other benefits may be seen as a success of the programme, but there are also likely to be negative effects of such sign-offs. For the individuals concerned, signing-on may have been a way of keeping in touch with the labour market. Claiming another benefit, such as a disability or carers benefit, might cause the person to lose contact with the world of work for a significant amount of time. There are implications for public expenditure too. The number of claimants of Invalidity/Incapacity Benefit trebled, from around 600,000 in 1979 to 1.79 million by 1997 and half of those receiving invalidity benefit in 1995 were previously unemployed (Guardian, 20/3/97).

So, the main effects of the six-month Restart interview were, in the short term, to increase sign-offs, and in the long term, to increase participation in employment and training programmes.

It is vital to note that these were the effects of Restart as it was being operated in 1989/90. At the time, although attendance at the actual Restart interview was compulsory, the menu of options was voluntary and there was a fair degree of choice offered to claimants. 11% of those attending the interview refused the offer of a programme place made to them by the adviser, and only one in seven of those were referred to adjudication for potential failure to meet the job seeking conditions attached to claiming benefit. In addition, another 10% of interview attenders were classed as 'offer not appropriate' i.e. they were not made an offer because there was no suitable offer on the menu, or the offer was withdrawn after it was found to be unsuitable (e.g. because the claimant had fallen ill).

Welfare-to-work and the long term unemployed

In the early 1990s there was increasing pressure on Restart advisers to achieve 'positive outcomes' and in 1994 a target was introduced for the ES requiring it to get 50% of claimants from the twelve month Restart interview, and 35% of claimants from their two year interview into a 'positive outcome'. Because "direct job outcomes are not easy to achieve from these interviews, the easiest way for ES staff to achieve a positive outcome initially was by ensuring that a claimant took up a place on a government programme" (Murray, 1997a, p. 16). It is not surprising therefore that between 1990/91 and 1994/95, the proportion of interviewees referred to a programme rose from 10% to 24% while the proportion placed in jobs only rose from 1% to 1.3% (ibid).

In 1996, the definition of a positive outcome was changed to exclude all government programmes with the exception of those that resulted in people moving off the register (mainly TfW). The result was an immediate increase in the proportion placed into jobs (as intended), although only to 4.5%. Another result, however was to cause a disturbing increase in the proportion of sign-offs 'for other reasons' (and these exclude starts on other benefits), from 3.6% to 9.7%, because sign-offs of this kind are counted as positive outcomes. Unless we make the unlikely assumption that all those involved were fraudulently it is hard, from the client's point of view, to see that signing off without entering a job, programme or other benefit might in any way be positive.

In addition, people who fail to take up an option at the 12, 18 or 24 month Restart interviews are now referred to either a compulsory job search programme or a series of intensive caseloading interviews, which has the effect of making the Restart options far less voluntary.

What these figures suggest is that Restart interviews have radically changed over time in three ways:

- finding options to suit claimant needs has been gradually replaced by targets for outcomes to be achieved by advisers;

- the menu of 'positive outcomes' being offered to claimants has been severely curtailed; and

- claimants are increasingly required to take up an option or face penalties.

It therefore cannot be assumed that the findings of The Restart Effect apply to the Restart process of today. They might, however, be relevant to attempts to build a more client-centred approach to tackling unemployment.

Jobsearch and the impact of Caseloading

As well as referring people to options, Restart had been intended to increase claimant's own job search activity. However, the authors of The Restart Effect did not find evidence that Restart increased levels of job search. Perhaps this is not surprising from a one-off interview. But the intensive caseloading programmes 1-2-1 and Jobfinder were introduced specifically to increase the level and effectiveness of claimants' job search, so we might expect them to have more significant effects on job outcomes.

They're very cynical

In fact the quantitative evidence is somewhat inconclusive. A small-scale pilot study was conducted in 1993/94 in North Norfolk to test the effects of an intensive caseloading programme for people who refused other options at a Restart interview. The results, using a control group study, seemed impressive. After six months, 22% of those who had been randomly assigned to caseloading interviews were in work, compared to only 8% of those who had not been assigned to caseloading (Birtwhistle et al, 1994).

However, the researchers warned that as the findings were based on the work of only four client advisers operating from two locations if the pilot was extended to other locations the "findings would be expected to vary from place to place and, as with any programme be subject to diminishing returns" (ibid, 3.5).

When 1-2-1 caseloading was extended this appears to be what happened. A larger pilot was carried out in 1994/95 in which a number of pilot ES offices referred to 1-2-1 all claimants who refused other options at the 12-month Restart interview. The control group comprised claimants signing on in other offices and they were referred to a Jobplan Workshop (see above), the normal national procedure at the time. The comparison was thus between 1-2-1 and Jobplan rather than between 1-2-1 and nothing. The evaluation found "no difference in effectiveness between 1-2-1 and Jobplan". Nevertheless, it was suggested that:

> The evaluation of Jobplan, for all ages, showed a positive register effect. It could therefore be inferred that 1-2-1 may also have a positive effect when compared to no intervention (Kay et al, 1995a, p. 3).

As discussed earlier, however, although Jobplan was found to have a small register effect, it was not shown to significantly increase the number of people finding work. It seems that the dramatic results achieved in the North Norfolk pilots was unusual and the gains disappeared when the programme was extended.

The only other control group study was that conducted on 1-2-1/Workwise, a programme for 18-24 year olds who refused other offers at the 12-month Restart interview. People in this situation were required to attend both 1-2-1 and a Workwise course. As discussed in the previous section the evaluation did find that 1-2-1/Workwise had a small but significant effect on job prospects and entry to training compared with no provision, and it also increased the likelihood of participants simply signing-off (Kay and Fletcher, 1996).

Welfare-to-work and the long term unemployed

Participants' opinions of Caseloading

Participant's opinions suggest that caseloading interviews, if resourced and delivered well, are found useful by some unemployed people, but compulsory caseloading often undermines the relationship between ES advisers and claimants.

The first Project Work pilots, aimed at those out of work for over two years, included an element of voluntary caseloading. A qualitative evaluation found that:

> those who had regular sessions with the same person were, in the main, very positive about the experience. They had appreciated both the continuity and the more intensive help they had had with their job search. Some also commented that they had felt encouraged by the interest shown in them and the feeling that the advisers really wanted to help them find work (Ritchie & Legard, 1997, p. 28).

In particular, these participants seemed to be using the interviews to gain information about jobs, training and other issues such as transport.

In the Project Work pilots, some people were offered 1-2-1 sessions but declined the offer. This was:

> largely because they thought there was little that the ES could provide that would be of help to them. In some cases this was because they were reasonably confident about their job search activity and felt they could be just as - if not more - effective left to their own devices. In other cases it was because their unproductive history of contact with client advisers had left them with little enthusiasm to make it more intensive. Amongst the latter group were clients who felt they had had a lot of pressure put on them to take what they thought were unsuitable jobs (ibid, p. 28-9).

This is clear evidence, confirmed also by our focus groups, of the adverse effect non client-centred contact with claimants can have on claimants' future attitudes to ES counselling.

Evidence about claimants' experiences of compulsory caseloading demonstrates these dangers. For example, of twelve people interviewed who had experienced at least two 1-2-1 interviews in the North Norfolk Pilots, three described the process as "a waste of time" and two others felt that "pressure was being brought to bear unreasonably" (CRG, 1994, p. 9). Only three of the twelve were described as having "no objections/positive reactions".

In general, the study concluded that "the compulsory nature [of 1-2-1] was not in itself an issue with claimants, it was the style of delivery which gave rise to complaints" (ibid, p. 32, original emphasis). While "some claimants experienced a positive and helpful approach from client advisers ... other experienced a more unsympathetic one". Claimants accepted and understood that the process "was there to satisfy the ... Jobcentre's needs as well as their own" but "dissatisfaction

They're very cynical

arose where the claimant thought the ... Jobcentre's needs were being satisfied at the expense of their own" (ibid, p. 9).

It is clear that many unemployed people do want access to impartial information and advice about job and training opportunities from a personal adviser. For example, a number of participants on job search courses suggested more personal interviews and one-to-one advice tailored to the needs of the individual (DVL Smith Ltd, 1994, p. 50; Blagg et al, 1994, p. 8). A qualitative study into claimant's attitudes about the ES also found that claimants were "particularly enthusiastic" about the idea of having a "named personal adviser at the Jobcentre". This would mean "a more personal service and someone to talk to about problems, not only to do with jobs and training, but also in relation to benefits and more general issues surrounding their future in work" (Cragg Ross and Dawson, 1993, p. 26).

On the other hand, sessions that are not based around achieving the claimant's own goals but instead try to force claimants into options they believe are unsuitable are unpopular and may jeopardise future relations between the claimant and the ES.

Caseloading interviews are perceived by ES staff to be most suitable "for those with clear goals who need information or job broking". Those requiring help with job hunting skills are likely to be better off on a job search course except for "a few individuals lacking the confidence for group participation" (Wright & Cooper, 1996, p. 5). Neither caseloading nor job search courses were thought to be suitable for those with "severe multiple problems".

Good practice guidelines

The qualitative evidence suggests a number of guidelines for good practice in delivering caseloading interviews:

- resources for caseloading need to be properly ring fenced, otherwise there is a danger of them being "reallocated to other target achieving duties, especially where there [are] severe staffing shortages", leading to staff just going "through the motions" of the caseloading process (Wright & Cooper, 1996);

- individuals undergoing a series of interviews should have the same adviser for each interview so that a relationship can be built up. Where this does not happen, participants get less out of the process and can be frustrated if they want to see the first adviser again (Ritchie & Legard, 1997, p. 28); and

- individuals should be given some time to consider their options before deciding, for example, to start on a programme. Some claimants have complained "that information was not available prior to interviews at the Jobcentre and that it was difficult to make snap decisions" (Cragg Ross and Dawson, 1993, p. 33).

The key issue, however, is to reduce the negative aspects of compulsion and to make caseloading interviews more client-centred. Although most unemployed people accept in principle, and indeed support, the conditions attached to benefit entitlement, including 'signing on' and compulsory attendance at Restart interviews, this must be applied fairly and balanced by attention to their individual circumstances and to their entitlement to positive individual support.

The credibility of ES advisers and interviews could also be strengthened if there was a reduction of 'target chasing'. If advisers have to hit targets for certain outcomes then inevitably the process loses the focus on the needs of the individual. Removing all outcome targets is too simplistic, but it should be possible to broaden the definition of acceptable positive outcomes. This could include jobs, all government programmes (not only ones involving removal from the register) and, crucially, participation in independent activities which improve long term job prospects such as voluntary work and part-time study or training. In effect the objective could shift from a crude job seeking activity test to a broader employment related participation test.

Job search resources and Jobclubs

Studies show that the lack of resources such as a car or telephone are major barriers to finding work. For example, a recent DSS research report found that someone without a telephone spends on average two and a half times as long on benefit than someone with a phone even after other factors such as social class and education are taken into account (Shaw et al, 1996, p. 135). In an earlier study, Daniel found that access to a car or motorbike reduced the amount of time it took men to get back into work by over a third (Daniel, 1990, p. 143).

Although these problems can only be effectively tackled through transport and communications policies the ES has provided programmes aimed at reducing the impact they have on job search activities. In particular, job seeking 'resource centres' have been created, especially through the Jobclub programme, and special assistance has been available to help pay for the costs associated with travelling to interviews outside the individual's home area.

Resource centres containing telephones, stationery, stamps, typewriters or word processors, relevant newspapers, books and journals have been available to people unemployed for more than six months since the mid-1980s when Jobclubs were introduced. Jobclub combines access to a resource centre with a structured induction session that is basically a job search course. Participation in Jobclubs is voluntary, although some unemployed people report that they have been put under pressure to attend.

The number of places in Jobclubs increased with rising unemployment in the early 1990s but has been declining broadly in line with claimant unemployment since 1995/96. At their peak in 1994/95 over a quarter of a million unemployed people made use of their facilities, falling to less than 200,000 in 1996/97. Reductions are planned to continue into 1998/99 when, in some parts of the

They're very cynical

country, Jobclubs will become part of programme centre provision (see below) (DfEE, 1998, p. 103).

Management information suggests that around 40% of Jobclub participants leave for a job, and external providers are paid on the basis of securing such outcomes. It is difficult to undertake control group studies of non-compulsory programmes, with the result that there has only been one such study of Jobclubs. This used a matched comparison group method, which is not as robust a method as a randomised trial so the results should be regarded with some caution (for a discussion of the shortcomings of this method see Appendix B).

The researchers measured the job outcomes (they did not consider other outcomes) of the pro- gramme group and the control group six months after entry to Jobclub. They found that Jobclub did improve the employment prospects of women and of men without vocational qualifications. Somewhat surprisingly, however, Jobclub actually worsened the employment prospects of men with vocational qualifications. In other words those in the non-assisted control group had signifi- cantly better outcomes than the programme group. Estimates of job entry rates net of deadweight (after six months) for each of these groups of participants were found to be as follows:

Women	15%
Men without vocational qualifications	10%
Men with vocational qualifications	-5%

These results suggest there are significant benefits resulting from Jobclub participation for women and unskilled men because these rates are considerably higher than those for job search courses or caseloading (although Jobclub does include a short job search course in the form of an induc- tion programme). For men, however, there is a downside, which is that Jobclub participants found jobs that paid on average 7% less than the jobs gained by the control group. This may not be so surprising as participants may have been more willing to consider lower wage rates and Jobclubs themselves encourage participants to be less selective about the quality of jobs applied for.

It should also be noted that specialist Jobclubs have been established for people with disabilities, ex-offenders, executives, people with literacy or numeracy problems and people from ethnic mi- norities, and, apart from executive Jobclubs, these usually have lower job entry rates than stand- ard Jobclubs.

Participant and staff opinions' of Jobclubs and Resource Centres

Job search resource centres are generally viewed favourably by unemployed people, as was confirmed by our focus group evidence. The 1994 ES Customer Satisfaction Survey showed that unemployed people rated Jobclub as the job search programme most likely to increase their job prospects. One survey of claimants found that Jobclub was the best known programme and:

> those who had used Jobclub were typically quite positive about it. They welcomed the availability of advice and information, and the access to materials it offered. A few thought it had had a tangible effect in helping them find work (Cragg, Ross and Dawson, 1993, p. 26).

Indeed, there is evidence that short-term unemployed people want access to their facilities and resent "the fact that Jobclub ... [is] only available to those out of work for six months or more" (Cragg Ross and Dawson, 1993, p. 26; see also NACAB, 1994, p. 27-29).

In terms of other 'resource' provision a qualitative study of Jobplan Workshops found that participants made positive comments about "the resources available particularly the computers, videos and literature" (Blagg et al, 1994, p. 18). However, a more extensive survey of Project Work, where participants had to undertake three hours job search per week, found that participants' experiences varied widely. Some describing it as a waste of time while others gave it high praise (Ritchie & Legard, 1997, p. 39-40). Participants mentioned three main factors determining the quality of provision:

- **the resources provided:** the most positive experiences were of offices with computers, telephones, envelopes, stamps, a wide selection of newspapers and even secretaries to type up CVs. Less positive experiences particularly related to out of date materials such as newspapers which were several days old. Where there was a board with jobs from the Jobcentre, people complained that they were mostly out of date and, because they had to stay on the providers' premises, they were not allowed to go to the Jobcentre to look at the latest vacancies.

- **staff:** participants liked having two or three staff on whom they could draw as a resource, for example for help with an application or information on the local labour market. Criticisms centred on lack of staff available to give personal help, or poor quality staff who didn't know what they were doing.

- **the mix of participants:** a number of participants complained that too broad a mix of people were in the group. Some people were far less able to undertake job search activities than others were, and literacy and numeracy problems were mentioned frequently in this regard. This mix led to frustration for the more able and embarrassment and sometimes 'anguish' for those with difficulties.

They're very cynical

Although the evidence shows that unemployed people can benefit from job search courses, and often appreciate gaining access to resource centres, the impact this has on their job prospects is mixed. It is also clear that compulsion and 'target chasing' have helped undermine claimants' confidence in ES staff.

At the same time the recent emphasis on job search programmes, coupled with reductions in other opportunities, has helped demotivate staff as well as the unemployed. A 1994 survey of staff attitudes revealed that in their view:

> the emphasis on jobsearch makes clients view our [the ES's] provision as repetitive and stale. Even popular and proven effective programmes like Jobclub seem 'tired' in the context of so much which focuses on improving jobseeking skills (Beattie, 1994, p. 8).

Staff were also concerned that there were so many different job search programmes with different names and eligibility requirements all offering much the same thing, with the result that claimants are confused abd fail to get full value from the provision on offer.

The development of Programme Centres

In 1996/97 the ES began to respond to the criticisms made by staff and unemployed people by piloting new 'programme centres' in eight areas. The idea was to move away from the provision of rigidly structured job search programmes, such as Jobclubs and Jobplan, and to deliver job search advice and guidance on a modular basis. The other aim of the new approach was to reduce the number of providers, which would help upgrade the staff skills and quality available by concentrating provision in a smaller number of larger centres.

The centre modules were adapted from existing programme sessions and include topics such as 'setting job goals', 'CV preparation', 'telephone techniques', 'coping with setbacks', etc. Centres have been encouraged to develop their modules over time, based on their own experience and feedback from participants and ES staff. Each of the centres also has resource areas where jobseekers attend regularly for agreed periods to actively apply for jobs and other opportunities. In the resource area the participants has access to continuing professional support and to phones, stamps, copiers, word processors, etc. Where necessary it may be possible for the centres to deliver outreach help to jobseekers in remote areas.

An evaluation of the centres, which interviewed ES Business Managers in six pilot areas, confirmed much of the research evidence about the problems with the previous approach to programme provision (Hamblin, 1997, p. 1-2):

- clients were obliged to do set courses regardless of their needs or of what they had already done on other schemes;

- the courses did not always run regularly and were often held on different sites spread over a wide area; and

- the fact that attendance was mandatory was thought to lead to a negative attitude on the part of attendees right from the start.

The managers also suggested that there were "large differences" between the standards of facilities and resources offered by providers; a lack of consistency between elements of courses; and the "administration of schemes was often poor". The problems were exacerbated by competition between providers leading to more "emphasis on achieving large turnouts than on positive outcomes".

The managers had high expectations of the new approach, the main one being the "greater flexibility of courses and the ability to tailor them to client needs, which in turn would make courses easier to sell". This would be backed by "a single, permanent site with good facilities/resources and offering greater problem counselling". It was expected that this would reduce confusion for both staff and clients as to which site to refer to/attend and also provide more immediate provision than was possible with the 'old' schemes. There was also an expectation that poor providers would be removed and that there would be an improvement in administration.

However, there was also concern about a number of potential problems, especially about travel to centres for those in outlying areas and liaison with more distant providers. There were also concerns about the ability of the providers to deliver the quality of service needed, and whether non-local providers "would understand the problems of the area they were working in".

The evaluation found that, "by and large", the positive expectations had been met and the negative ones proved to be unfounded. It seemed that because advisers had been able to select those modules they thought were appropriate to clients it had been easier to 'sell' attendance and the number of people volunteering had increased. Many of the centres had been flexible enough to adjust start times of modules to when clients are able to reach the centre via public transport In addition, the single permanent site, as well as making it less confusing about where clients should be sent, were offering good facilities in high standard buildings. Immediate provision was generally available and the centres provided a continuous point of contact where there is usually someone on hand to help clients with problems. Centres had also been bringing in outside agencies to offer advice on debt and health problems. At the same time the problems had not been as great

They're very cynical

as envisaged. Providers had performed well and "clients in most areas .. appeared to be more willing to travel than expected".

Local ES advisers used a variety of referral procedures and were not given particular training in how to select modules. This was initially daunting for some but confidence increased over time, often supported by liaison with programme centre staff. Where there was a choice of centre the decision was made either on the basis of which one was easier to access or which was next running the appropriate module. In "both instances the clients' wish was the major deciding factor".

Apart from problems with one centre the ES Business managers concluded that overall the centres were "a big improvement on previous schemes". The main reason is the ability to tailor assistance "which is more satisfying for the staff and is apparently also appreciated by the clients".

There was limited feedback from unemployed people in the evaluation but it seemed that clients particularly appreciated the fact that the Jobcentre "is taking greater note of their individual requirements and not forcing them into a scheme with no thought of whether it is needed or not" (ibid, p. 3). This was reinforced by better quality resources and staff at the centres' who were more professional and "more attentive to clients' needs" than had been the case with previous provision. The unemployed people who attended enjoyed being "treated more like adults" and because the provision was "seen to be run by an outside agency and not by 'government' seemed to make them more relaxed and receptive".

In all areas clients were referred voluntarily at least once but if they did not attend then they were mandated. In most districts it seemed that far fewer people were being mandated to attend the programme centre than under the old regime, though in "deprived" areas there was still considerable resistance to "another scheme" and there were just as many mandatory referrals in some of these areas as before. Not surprisingly voluntary clients were more positive than mandated ones.

There were some problems over mixing mandated and voluntary clients together as the former "tended to be more negative and to hinder the learning process for the others". Some providers thought it was possible to use their skills to enable both groups to work together, though others thought that "disruptive clients" should not be included in the modules and that other provision should be found. One other major problem was that mandated participants did not enjoy any flexibility about modules and were required to take what was on offer on the days they were required to attend.

The ES plans to extend the programme centre approach and in 1998/99 ES Districts have been given the freedom "where their local partners agree" to use the funding available for Jobclubs and Jobplan to develop local centres. The centres will have to cater for the jobseekers mandated to attend Jobplan, who will have to attend for a full week, "but the content of the week need not follow thew Jobplan syllabus" (Employment Service, 1998, p. 3).

Welfare-to-work and the long term unemployed

Although the programme centre approach could represent a significant advance there is as yet no evidence that it actually helps people obtain jobs quicker. There is also no guarantee that the positive impact of the initial pilots will be maintained as provision is expanded and as more mixing takes place between voluntary and mandated participants.

Assistance with travel to interview costs

Financial assistance has been available for many years to unemployed people wishing to attend interviews outside their home areas. The current programme, which has been in existence since 1986, is the Travel to Interview Scheme (TIS). It covers travel costs and unavoidable overnight accommodation for unemployed people who are attending interviews beyond 'normal daily travelling distance' from their home. Provision peaked with just over 50,000 participants in 1994/95, falling to just under 40,000 participants in 1997/98.

The logic behind the programme is clear. Firstly, by assisting individuals in areas of high unemployment to apply for jobs in areas with lower unemployment, their chances of finding work are improved. Secondly, by increasing the geographical mobility of the labour force, skill shortages in particular areas can be reduced encouraging inflation-free growth.

Financial assistance is required because research shows that "many employers do not meet the travelling expenses of interview candidates, which places those on benefits at a great disadvantage in the job market" (Finn, 1995, p. 6). A 1992 survey of 3,000 employers found that over half did not repay travel costs for candidates attending an interview and about two thirds did not normally meet accommodation and subsistence costs (Atkinson & Hillage, 1993).

There have been no control group studies of TIS that provide a reliable and comparable estimate of job entry rates net of deadweight. The most recent study (Bryson, 1995) does, however, provide some evidence about the effectiveness of TIS. The study examined relaxations to the programme's eligibility conditions which were being piloted, and most of which were extended to the national scheme in 1996. The main changes were: abolishing the £25,000 salary limit for eligible vacancies; extending help to second and subsequent interviews; and introducing a more flexible approach to temporary jobs.

The study suggested that TIS does increase the number of people taking jobs in other areas of the country. Nearly one in five (18%) of those who received help with their costs got the jobs they applied for. Of these, a quarter (24%) said that they would not have applied for the job or would not have attended the interview without assistance from the scheme. This is not an accurate deadweight figure, because it relies on the opinions of participants.

The scheme particularly assisted those applying for skilled and relatively well paid vacancies. The study found that average wages of the jobs applied for were £15,400 (in 1994/95) and 53% were managerial, professional or associate professional.

They're very cynical

The significance of these findings are twofold. On the one hand, TIS is a programme which is of most use to skilled unemployed people, who are already on average less disadvantaged in the labour market. On the other hand, it is likely to assist in the reduction of skill shortages which means that it can be expected to have lower substitution and displacement than other job search programmes. In other words, people being assisted to take skilled jobs elsewhere will not simply be replacing other potential employees. Instead they will help employers in areas of skill shortage to recruit staff without having to raise wages and help fuel inflationary pressures.

TIS is also popular with participants. A review by NACAB of their clients' experiences of Government programmes for the unemployed concluded that "there is no doubt about the usefulness of the scheme, but this is severely limited by the numerous eligibility criteria" (NACAB, 1994, p. 11). Some of these criteria were relaxed in the 1996 changes, but one requirement in particular was actually made stricter. Before 1996, all those out of work for over four weeks were eligible for assistance. In 1996 eligibility was restricted to those unemployed for over thirteen weeks, and also restricted to the claimant unemployed only, thus excluding other groups such as women returners.

The restriction to the three-month plus unemployed was not piloted along with the other changes. Indeed, the evaluation study found that the programme was particularly effective for people who had only been unemployed for a short time. Just over one in five (21%) of TIS recipients unemployed for less than thirteen weeks got the job, compared with only 11% of those unemployed longer. The short-term unemployed were also more likely to report that they would not have applied for the job or attended the interview without assistance. The author concluded that TIS appears to encourage "more people with very short spells of unemployment (less than 13 weeks) to apply and accept jobs they would not otherwise have considered" (Bryson, 1995, p. 4).

Another problem with the scheme is that it has a limited budget which means that staff are responsible for restricting access to the assistance (even among those who meet the eligibility criteria), which inevitably is a somewhat arbitrary process. The Unemployment Unit has received reports that in some local Jobcentres money is allocated on a monthly basis and runs out in the first few days of each month.

In general the evidence suggests that assistance with travel to interview costs has a positive role to play as part of an active labour market policy aimed at creating sustainable employment growth without inflation. Because it is mainly useful to those with higher skills, it could perhaps be combined with education and training programmes to help people get skills and then find jobs to use those skills. Although there will always only be a limited number of unemployed people who are able and willing to move home to take work, it does appear that the programme could be usefully expanded to help more people. It is worth noting that the cost per place is low at only £26 in 1997/98 and that the total annual cost of TIS is only £1 million, which is equivalent to under 2% of the total spending on job search programmes.

There are two main ways in which this assistance could be expanded effectively:

- remove the 13 week eligibility condition; and

- review the definition of daily travelling distance and expand provision in areas of high unemployment.

Trying to go further than this by restricting assistance to people applying for jobs in areas of skill shortage is probably so complex that it would undermine the effectiveness of the scheme. Indeed TIS was specifically introduced because it was found in a pilot study to be a "simpler scheme to operate" than the more targeted programmes it replaced (Lourie, 1997, p. 50).

The one problem that TIS does not address is the travel costs and inadequate transport services which still blight the job prospects of many of the long term unemployed in their local labour markets, especially in rural areas. One solution could be to provide assistance to those in genuine need in areas of high unemployment to access job vacancies in what are now classified as their local labour markets enabling, for example, some of the long term unemployed in inner London boroughs to approach employers in central London. Another option is to build on the travel concessions which some transport companies are now giving to the younger unemployed people in the New Deal for 18 to 24 year olds.

Lack of recent work experience is itself one of the many barriers to work faced by unem ployed people, particularly the long-term unemployed. A survey by the Institute for Employment Studies of 800 business leaders found that 56% of employers think peo ple's skills deteriorate the longer they are out of work and 54% think work attitudes and discipline also suffer (Atkinson et al, 1996).

It is important not to overstate this barrier. 77% of respondents to the same survey said that it was no more risky to take on someone unemployed than someone in work. Also, while it is true that long term unemployed people have lower chances of getting work than the short term unemployed recent evidence indicates that this is likely to be caused by the characteristics they started with. People who experience barriers to employment such as lack of skills are much more likely to become long term unemployed than those without such barriers (see Nimmo, 1996; Webster, 1997).

A large scale study of the factors which affected people's chances of leaving Income Support (Shaw et al, 1996) found that those who had done any paid work in the two years before starting benefit took on average only half as long to leave benefit as those who had not worked. This effect was significant, although dwarfed by the effects of other crucial factors such as qualifications, access to resources, and personal characteristics such as ethnicity and gender.

There are several ways in which Government has tried to enable the long term unemployed to acquire recent and relevant work experience. The first has involved funding short-term jobs in the public or not-for-profit sectors of the economy. The second method has involved paying businesses to take on unemployed people through employment subsidies. The third approach has been to allow unemployed people and employers to assess the suitability of a job or applicant through Work Trials.

Temporary work programmes

Government run temporary work programmes have been a part of British labour market policy since the late 1970s. They have been targeted at the long-term unemployed and typically provide participants with work placements on projects of benefit to the local community; from environ- mental or landscaping schemes, through to projects providing services for children, young peo- ple, the elderly and people with disabilities. In the 1970s they were small-scale counter-cyclical measures aimed at providing temporary relief until labour demand improved. In the mid-1980s there was a dramatic expansion and the Community Programme, with over 250,000 participants at its peak, was used to help reduce the unemployment count and manage the crisis of long term unemployment. In 1988 temporary work programmes were scrapped in favour of Employment Training, though temporary work programmes were again introduced as unemployment increased in the early 1990s.

There are a range of complex issues which characterise debates about the use of temporary work programmes. They do help provide jobs where opportunities do not exist in local labour markets, though they also generate fierce debates about displacement and substitution, especially when implemented on the scale of the 1980s Community Programme. The programmes can also pro- duce substantial community benefits, though there have been no serious evaluations of the value of such benefits. They also have the potential, when implemented imaginatively, to help stimulate job creation in the social economy (CLES, 1996).

However, one of the major concerns about temporary work programmes is that they encourage participants to give up active job search, and have sometimes offered people better options than were available in the local jobs market. This concern underpins three key trends in temporary work experience programmes, all of which have been designed to improve work incentives. Firstly, the earlier programmes paying participants the hourly rate for the job were replaced by programmes paying an allowance equivalent to the level of 'benefit-plus' £10 a week. Secondly, the duration of Government programmes has fallen from the one-year placements available on CP, to the six months available under Employment Action, to the thirteen weeks provided under Project Work. Thirdly, voluntary participation was replaced with compulsory attendance in 1996 with the ending of Community Action and the introduction of the first Project Work pilots.

The flagship programme of the new Labour government, the New Deal for 18 to 24 year olds, continues the trend towards compulsory attendance. It also relies heavily on work experience programmes provided either in the voluntary or environmental sectors, usually paying benefit plus £15 a week, or through employment subsidies, where participants should receive the normal rate for the job. The key innovation with the new Government's approach is to integrate day release training into all its work experience programmes.

The impact of temporary work programmes

There is mixed evidence about the impact that temporary work programmes have on future job prospects. Between 20% and 30% of participants are typically in work three to six months after leaving the programme. In addition, another 5% to 10% are in other 'positive outcomes' such as full-time education or government training.

These outcomes inevitably include significant elements of deadweight. The only rigorous control group study of a British temporary work programme was of Employment Action, a relatively small programme (about 50,000 starts per year) which ran between 1991 and 1993 and was available

They're very cynical

to people who had been continuously unemployed for at least six months. It ran alongside the larger scale Employment Training programme and was therefore aimed at those for whom "training is neither necessary nor appropriate" (NCVO News, October 1994). It offered work experience placements of up to six months duration, mainly on projects run by voluntary organisations, combined with an element of job search.

The study (Payne et al, 1996) used a matched comparison method (see Appendix B) and found that participation in Employment Action had little effect on job prospects. After controlling for the effects of other characteristics, participants were no more likely to have entered work than the control group at 18, 24 and 30 months after the start of the period of unemployment that qualified them for the programme. Although there was found to be a small positive effect by three years after the start of the qualifying spell of unemployment (32% of participants had entered work at some point compared with 28% of non-participants), the authors warn that "the estimates for long durations after the start of the qualifying spell of unemployment are less robust than the estimates for short durations" (ibid, p. 31). In any case, this small positive effect did not translate into a greater overall duration in employment over the two-year survey period (ibid, p. 38).

It was found, however, that the longer a person stayed on the programme the more likely they were to find a job afterwards leading the authors to conclude that "project placements only improved job chances if scheme participants stayed on them for a long time" (ibid, intro, 5).

There is also evidence that the compulsory temporary work programme Project Work may have increased the number of people signing off, many of whom claimed sickness benefits. The qualitative evaluation of the programme found that "for some it certainly appeared that Project Work had heightened their awareness of an existing condition for which they then received a medical statement" and that for others their experience of Project Work led them to simply leave the register (Ritchie & Legard, 1997, p. 59). The authors cite the example of a women in her late forties who stopped claiming just before being referred to work experience:

> She expected to have to do manual work on her placement. She suffers from high blood pressure and vertigo and felt she would be quite unable to do so. She said she felt very 'frightened' because she did not know where she was going or what she would be doing. She got a sick note for a short while but eventually decided to come off the register altogether. She is now reliant on her family for financial support (ibid, p. 60).

The lack of positive evidence that temporary work programmes improve future job prospects is not to say that they have no part to play within a range of provision to unemployed people. It should be stressed that the control group study discussed above was a study of a benefit-plus programme with no training attached. There is evidence that programmes that combine work experience, which pays a wage, with training may achieve significantly better outcomes. This approach is central to local strategies that have aimed to create what is described as an 'Intermediate Labour Market'.

Intermediate Labour Market programmes

During the 1990s a number of local employment programmes have been developed which aim to improve the employability of long-term unemployed people by creating an 'Intermediate Labour Market' (ILM) to act as a bridge between unemployment and the mainstream labour market. The programmes are significant because they offered a workable alternative to the last Government's approach and also because this model for delivering temporary work is being adapted in the new Government's pilot Employment Zones and is also being used in some areas as part of the New Deal for the young unemployed.

ILMs have a number of defining characteristics (CLES, 1996):

- participation is voluntary;

- participants are paid rate for the job and are treated as regular employees e.g. they can be sacked for misconduct;

- training is a core element of the time spent on the programme; and

- the work undertaken is 'real work' which is of clear benefit to the community. Examples are insulation of council houses, reforestation and child care provision.

The two best known ILM programmes are those provided by Glasgow Works and the Wise Group (which is based in Glasgow but has local equivalents in a number of other areas). The projects usually offer participants up to a year of paid work and training.

The ILM approach has been developed as a specific response to local problems and usually as an alternative to mainstream Government provision, though some elements of national programmes are drawn on by the ILM initiatives.

Comparing ILMs and government temporary work programmes

ILM programmes appear to cost far more than mainstream temporary work schemes, but providers claim that if all factors are taken into account they offer better value for money. In practice, it is difficult to make comparisons between ILM programmes and government work experience programmes, for a number of reasons.

The gross cost of a one year ILM programme is around £11,000 to £14,000 per entrant, which includes all costs: wages of staff and participants, training costs, work materials and overheads. The simplest and most reliable comparison with a mainstream government programme would be with the Community Programme because it offered twelve months of paid work experience. It cost about £10,000 per entrant at 1997 prices, which suggests that ILM programmes are slightly

They're very cynical

more expensive, perhaps reflecting the provision of training and the fact that ILM programmes tend to offer longer hours of work than did the Community Programme.

Making a comparison with recent government work experience programmes is much harder. They tend to cost around £2,000 per entrant, which is obviously far cheaper than ILM programmes, but this needs to be qualified. A number of adjustments need to be made to the ILM cost to make it comparable with this figure:

1   Public accounting procedures mean that the £2,000 figure excludes the cost of paying participants their benefit-plus allowances and passported benefits such as Housing and Council Tax Benefits, free prescriptions, etc. All these costs to the public purse are saved when unemployed people participate in paid work experience (although some in-work benefits may be payable). In addition, tax revenues are generated, creating further savings for the Treasury. This reduces the cost of an ILM programme significantly, by anything between £4,000 and £8,000 depending on the way in which the calculation is undertaken and the levels of benefits previously received by participants (see for example, McGregor et al, 1997, p. 61; Cambridge Policy Consultants, 1996, page ix).

2   ILM programmes offer up to a year of work experience compared with six months for recent government programmes. For a fairer comparison, the ILM cost should be halved.

These two adjustments bring down the cost of an ILM programme to between £2,000 to £5,000 per entrant which again suggests that ILM programmes are on average more expensive than government work experience programmes which pay benefit-plus and offer no training, but not by nearly as much as the gross costs suggest.

The outcomes participants achieve after leaving ILM programmes, on the other hand, appear to be dramatically better than those achieved by participants on mainstream government work experience programmes. Table 2 provides a comparison between the outcomes of national temporary work programmes and Wise Group projects.

The Wise Group's relative success could of course be due to differences in the intake to the programmes. However, enough information is available to test for the likely effects of two differences in intake: length of unemployment and age. Table 2 suggests that controlling for length of unemployment does reduce the advantage shown by the Community Programme over Community Action, but actually improves the relative performance of the Wise Group.

Outcomes by age are not available for the Wise Group programme, but it is at least possible to compare the intake of each programme by age as in Table 3. Older unemployed people find it harder to find work so a programme with a younger intake is likely to achieve better job outcomes.

Welfare-to-work and the long term unemployed

Table 3 does suggest that Community Action participants were significantly older than on the ILM programme, which means that its low job outcomes may be more of an achievement than suggested by the raw data. The Community Programme on the other hand was heavily skewed towards young recruits, probably because of the low wages it offered.

It may be that due to its intake of younger and shorter term unemployed people, the Community Programme did not in fact improve participants' future job prospects much more than Community Action despite the fact that the Community Programme offered a year of paid employment. The Wise group, on the other hand, although it targets a somewhat younger age group than Community Action, does seem to have achieved significantly better outcomes than the other programmes.

It is too early to draw firm conclusions, however. There is a need for a rigorous control group study into the effects of ILMs. The Wise Group has too many applicants for the jobs it offers so it has the chance to select applicants including by interview. It does not appear to be simply 'creaming' off the best candidates in terms of duration of unemployment or skill levels, but creaming may still be occurring in terms of other barriers to employment (e.g. ethnicity, resources, personal characteristics) and in terms of the levels of motivation to get a job displayed by participants.

Secondly, the results to date have been achieved by small-scale programmes. It is not clear that the ILM model could be expanded quickly into a national programme for the long-term unemployed without outcome rates falling significantly. Finally, it should be remembered that ILMs suffer from the same problems of substitution and displacement as other work experience programmes.

Nevertheless, the Glasgow experience with the ILM model does suggest that a voluntary programme offering real jobs combined with quality training can have significantly more impact on participants' employment prospects than other work experience programmes for only slightly higher net costs

Table 2: Employment outcomes of work experience programmes

Proportion in employment or self-employment(full or part time) at time of survey*

Programme	Description	All	Unemployed 1 year+	Unemployed 2years+
Wise Group Glasgow	Rate for the job work plus training for 12 months (ILM)	46%	46%	44%
Community Programme	Rate for the job work for 12 months	32%	26%	No data
Community Action	Benefit-plus work experience for 6 months	19%	19%	15%

*3 months after leaving Community Action; 6 months after leaving Wise Group; an average of 7 months after leaving Community Programme

Sources: McGregor et al (1997); Public Attitude Surveys Ltd (1997); Manpower Services Commission (1984)

Table 3: Proportion of surveyed participants by age

	Proportion of participants aged:	
Programme	18-24	45+
Wise Group Glasgow	34%	12%
Community Programme	52%	No data
Community Action	19%	28%

Sources: as for Table 3 plus Bryson (1995a)

Welfare-to-work and the long term unemployed

Participants' opinions of temporary work programmes

Participants have expressed a number of concerns about temporary work programmes, although these differ significantly between people on voluntary programmes and on compulsory schemes.

On voluntary programmes, the key concerns were the short duration of the programmes and the lack of training. A 1986 sample of Community Programme participants found that "for at least a third of participants the major criticism was that the one year scheme did not last long enough" (Finn, 1998, p. 21). Several reasons were given for this criticism:

- a year (particularly a year of part-time work) was considered "far too short to get proper experience", a point which reinforces the finding from the Employment Action study (see above) which found that the longer participants stayed on a placement the better their job chances afterwards;

- many participants felt that the programme had got their hopes up and given them an alternative to unemployment but that it would be extremely hard to face going back on the dole if they didn't get a job at the end. Participants used terms like "soul destroying" and "dread" to describe their feelings about ending the placement without a job to go to. This is supported by evidence from those who have returned to unemployment after participation on Project Work among whom "the general mood was one of disenchantment, sometimes accompanied by feelings of having been 'used' or given 'false hopes'" (Ritchie & Legard, 1997, p. 50); and

- projects in the social care field often provided services to vulnerable groups such as the elderly and disabled and the high turnover of project workers was extremely disruptive and even damaging to the clients.

The lack of training was a complaint of those on both voluntary and compulsory programmes. 10% of Community Programme participants interviewed specifically suggested that there should be proper structured training on the programme. Both participants and providers of places for the pilot work experience programme North Norfolk action saw the lack of formal training as "an inherent opportunity missed" (CRG, 1994, p. 33). The same was true of Project Work, on which "those who had hoped the placements would bring at least some training or skill enhancement were most bitterly disappointed" (Ritchie & Legard, 1997, p. 37).

Despite these complaints, many participants have been positive about voluntary temporary work programmes, often finding the actual work rewarding and reporting learning new skills and gaining experience.

Over 70% of Community Programme participants "thought that participation .. had increased their chance of getting a job" (Finn, 1998, p. 17) and nearly half (49%) of Community Action participants were 'very satisfied' with the work experience element of the programme, with another 31% being 'fairly satisfied' (Labour Market Quarterly Report, November 95, p. 15). 28% of CP participants found the work to be "worthwhile, rewarding or interesting"; 31% had enjoyed the work, especially the company of fellow workers; and 13% reported that "participation boosted their confidence and self-respect, and in several cases relieved them from the chronic depression and isolation they had been experiencing whilst unemployed" (Finn, 1988). Participants on North Norfolk Action found that participants liked the programme because it gave them something to do, provided a structure to the day, allowed them to "maintain work-related skills and possibly learn some new ones" and gave them the opportunity to work with others.

Even the compulsory Project Work programme, which was viewed extremely negatively by many participants, managed to provide some participants with positive experiences, particularly when they felt that the work was both worthwhile and interesting (Ritchie & Legard, p. 35-7).

These positive experiences also had an impact on people's activities and ambitions after the programme. For example, a few Project Work participants "had found the placement activity so rewarding, that they had chosen to carry on as a volunteer" (ibid, p. 50). This is evidently the case with other temporary work programmes too and increased participation in voluntary work may be a significant effect of these programmes. For example, 22% of ex-Community Action participants were doing voluntary work three months after leaving the programme (Public Attitude Surveys, 1997, p. 1), which compares with an estimate of 8% of all claimants undertaking voluntary work (Bottomley et al, 1997, p. 127).

A few participants decided to look for work in the occupational areas in which they had worked on their placement (Ritchie & Legard, 1997, p. 50), although many others "pointed to the shortage of vacancies in the unskilled or social care areas they were working in" (Finn, 1997, p. 18).

Good practice guidelines on temporary work provision

Qualitative studies point to a number of important criteria for ensuring that participants get most benefit from temporary work programmes.

The first involves **ensuring that there is a broad range of relevant work activity**. There were two features of Project Work "about which people were persistently critical at the outset and largely remained so throughout the course of the programme". One was being forced to work for their benefit ; the other was "the limited range of work experience on offer". In the main, participants:

> saw the placements as providing no opportunity to enhance their employment potential. The work they did had no intrinsic 'job value' to the participants, would add little of relevance to a CV and, perhaps most crucially, offered no opportu-

nity for learning or skill enhancement of any relevance (Ritchie & Legard, 1997, p. 20).

Project Work was the worst example of this, but there were participants on the Community Programme for example who made similar criticisms (Finn, 1988, p. 18). Evidence from a follow up survey of Community Action participants illustrates the importance of participants being committed to the work they do on placement. Of those who had been "very happy" or "fairly happy" with the type of work they were doing while on the programme, 21% and 17% respectively were in work three months after the programme. On the other hand of the 29 participants interviewed who were "not very happy" or "not at all happy" with the work, none had got a job.

The problem stems mainly from the prevalence of unskilled work and particularly manual work on programmes of this kind. Some found the work "useless or demeaning". Some felt that manual work was "wholly unsuitable for them" (on some occasions on health grounds). Some just found it boring, particularly if there was not enough work to be done. Indeed there were a "number of comments about standing around a lot, not having enough to do or constant cups of coffee". The greatest criticisms of the nature of the work on Project Work were from those who "saw the work as completely irrelevant to their own spheres of employment interest" (Ritchie & Legard, 1997, p. 37).

This is a major problem confronting temporary work programmes. The answer is to provide as wide a range of placements as possible, covering different occupational areas and levels, and to integrate training relevant to an individuals chosen area of work. The difficulty is that this increases costs, is hard to organise, and could help create a parallel labour market which offers opportunities and conditions more attractive than those available in the real job market.

With Project Work, the problem was that although there was a range of placements to begin with, as programme places began to fill up, there was very little choice left. The result was that some participants "had a quite extensive and varied list to choose from and were able to select something which had at least some appeal" but for others the list was far more limited, and often contained nothing the participant felt was appropriate. Finally, there were some who "were given no choice at all and were told what they would be doing". Those who had "very restrictive choice or none at all were very critical of this feature of the placement process" and these negative feelings "continued well into their placements" (ibid, p. 34) and were hard for providers to deal with (p. 76).

Secondly, participants should be treated with respect and equity. The way in which participants are treated by their host organisations and placement supervisors has been found to have "a fundamental effect on the participants' assessments" of temporary work placements. While "some felt they were treated with respect and some dignity, other said they felt demeaned, disregarded or looked upon as if they were 'criminals'". While "some talked about the civility and responsiveness of their supervisors, others said that they were treated like children or 'idiots' (ibid, p, 37).

The quality of supervisors is crucial to the success of a programme. If there is "inadequate, incompetent or even hostile supervision" this will "add to negative feelings about the 'usefulness' or ill judged value" of the placements (ibid).

Health and safety is also important and poor conditions on placements increase negative perceptions of temporary work programmes. The Project Work evaluation uncovered "descriptions, sometimes rather alarming, of poor or old tools, unsuitable equipment, the lack of protective or 'wet weather' clothing, of old, uninsured or unsafe transport and poor or non-existent fire regulations, or preventative equipment" (ibid, p. 38).

A clear and effective referral process is also significant. Many of the problems discovered by the Project Work evaluation relate to the process by which participants were referred to a work experience placement. Referral was via a number of 'providers' who acted as intermediaries between the ES and actual work placements. Providers were responsible for finding suitable work placements with voluntary organisations. The ES would then refer participants to a provider who would then have to find them a placement.

This system, combined with the compulsory nature of Project Work, proved to severely restrict the choice of placements given to some participants and was criticised by participants, ES staff and providers alike. The key to the problem was that ES staff could only refer each participant to a provider, not an actual placement. This meant that although they could allow participants to pick a provider thought to provide placements doing work the participant would find suitable, there was no guarantee that the provider would actually have that type of placement available at the time. ES staff expressed "regret that they had such little influence over matching their clients with suitable placements" (ibid, p. 69).

In addition, some providers were more popular than others were, but "because of the need to ensure an appropriate allocation of clients to each provider" some clients had to be sent to other providers with the result that "it was not always possible to offer any choice" (ibid, p. 68). There are some pragmatic ways of minimising these negative effects. These include (ibid, p. 80):

● increasing the 'lead time' between the ES referring a client to the provider and the provider being required to find a placement, so that providers have time to find a suitable placement;

● improving communication between ES staff and providers so that providers can find placements to suit client needs before referral, and ES staff can tell participants exactly what placements each provider currently has; and

● best of all, having the ES refer participants directly to a placement, without being referred to the provider first. Providers could still have a role in finding placements and acting as a link between the ES and organisations hosting placements, but from the unemployed person's point of view referral would be a seamless one-stage process.

Welfare-to-work and the long term unemployed

'Rate for the Job' versus 'benefit-plus'

There is clear evidence that most unemployed people involved in work programmes would prefer to be paid a 'proper wage' and that the move to 'benefit-plus' damaged the credibility of Government schemes which are seen by some as nothing more than 'cheap' or 'skivvy labour'. For example, a 1990 review of research studies touching on unemployed people's attitudes to programmes found (Department of Employment, 1990, para 15):

- a general feeling that participants are used as 'cheap labour' and that the pay or allowance received whilst on the schemes is insufficient to justify participation; and

- that "social representations of government schemes circulating within communities tend to revolve around notions of exploitation rather than genuine assistance".

This applies particularly (but not exclusively - see Finn, 1988) to benefit-plus schemes. A 1994 survey of ES staff discovered:

> *a common view that [Community Action] is less acceptable to clients than the old Community Programme used to be, primarily because "on Community Programme they got a wage in the wage packet, just like employed people. It might not have been much more than Unemployment Benefit plus £10 but the point was that it was a real pay packet for doing real work" (Beattie, 1994, p. 12).*

This is one of the reasons that ILM projects are popular with the unemployed. An evaluation of Wise group participants found that two thirds of leavers interviewed thought that the programme was better than other government training programmes with "the fact that the [programme] paid a wage the most commonly cited... single reason" (McGregor et al, 1997, p. 48).

A survey of participants on North Norfolk Action, a pilot work experience programme, reported that the £10 top-up is widely believed to be barely sufficient even to meet the costs associated with participation, including "travel costs and other out of pocket expenses e.g. wear and tear on clothes, etc." (CRG, 1994, p. 15).

A qualitative survey of the opinions of Project Work participants, who were required to participate in temporary work, found they were highly critical of the £10 allowance:

> *At the simplest level, there was criticism that the amount does not cover the additional expenses that were incurred by participating in the work placements. But there was much more vociferous complaint about the inadequacy of the payment as a return for the 'compulsory' work they were being made to do. Some of the participants felt that they would regard [the work placements] in a quite different light if they were adequately compensated for the work they had to do. The suggested level at which the allowance would be 'adequate' varied*

They're very cynical

from £20 to £50. It was also suggested that it would be preferable to have the money paid weekly 'like a wage', rather than on a fortnightly basis like 'signing on'.

Compulsory participation in work experience programmes is only likely to have credibility with unemployed people if the work offers a reasonable financial incentive and if it is of high quality.

However, the question of whether programmes should pay a wage or benefit-plus is not a simple one. The Community Programme, even though it offered the rate for the job, offered mainly low paid unskilled work, and the limited funding available meant that the majority of places were part-time. As a result, many CP places were "only financially attractive to single people living at home" (Finn, 1986, p. 4). The proportions of single people and of young people on the programme gradually grew. By 1985, nearly two thirds of entrants to the programme were aged between 18 and 25.

Since the 1980s, benefit traps have become more severe for many people due to rising housing costs (see Nimmo, 1997) with the result that part-time work is even less financially attractive to the majority of the unemployed, and the long-term unemployed in particular. The level of wages people will require in order to be better off on a programme than on benefit depends on the circumstances of the individual and on local housing costs (see Nimmo, 1997a). It is therefore the case that programmes paying a wage will be more successful in some local areas than in others.

Both these points are well illustrated by the experience of the Wise Group programmes. After a period on benefit-plus, participants are given the choice of being paid rate for the job or receiving benefit plus £10. In Glasgow, only 5% of participants choose benefit-plus whereas in Newham in London local rents are so high that by 1995 the Newham Wise programme was operating with over two-thirds of participants on benefit-plus. The tendency to stay on benefit-plus is also greatest among older trainees "reflecting their greater household responsibilities and the higher associated benefits". (McGregor et al, 1997, p. 19-20).

There are also problems with paying wages if programme jobs are only short term (e.g. six months) because participants have to sign off benefit in order to start on the programme and then have to re-claim not only Jobseeker's Allowance but also Housing Benefit and Council Tax Benefit at the end of the programme (unless they secure a job), a process which can cause severe interruption to household income.

Giving participants the choice, supported by access to in-depth benefit counselling and an individual 'better off' calculation by a suitably trained welfare rights worker, seems to be the best policy. It is also clear that £10 (or even £15 as paid on the New Deal) is likely to be considered by some, if not most, unemployed people to be far from sufficient.

Welfare-to-work and the long term unemployed

Employment subsidies

The object of employment subsidies is to induce employers to recruit the unemployed by offering them cash payments or tax rebates. In the UK there have been many subsidy schemes that have usually been aimed at the young and long-term unemployed. However, the last national subsidy programme, the New Workers Scheme, was wound up in 1989, and the last Government had only subsequently experimented with various Workstart pilot subsidy schemes.

The Labour Government has put the use of direct employment subsidies, aimed primarily at the private sector, at the heart of its New Deals for the young and long term unemployed. It is expected that about 40% of the 18 to 25 year old unemployed to be given programme assistance under the New Deal will be helped through six-month employment subsidies of £60 a week. In June 1998 employment subsidies of £75 a week for six months will be made available to about 15% of unemployed people who have been out of work for over two years.

The architects of the New Deal consider subsidised temporary job placements in the private sector to be generally preferable to temporary work programmes. As the Employment Policy Institute points out employment subsidies appear relatively more attractive for two reasons (1997, pp 69-76). First, it is suggested that by placing people in 'regular' jobs, temporary employment subsidies offer a superior form of work experience and training and are more likely to lead to real jobs. Secondly, the Government simply has to fund a payment to employers rather than cover the full cost (including supervision and materials) of employing people on temporary work programmes.

There have been numerous evaluations of the impact of the various employment subsidy schemes that were introduced in the 1970s and 1980s, and the evidence has been well documented and assessed by the Employment Policy Institute (1997). Considerable attention has also been given to the lessons that can be drawn from subsidy programmes in other countries and much of this evidence has been summarised and assessed in a report from the Education and Employment Select Committee of the House of Commons (ESC, 1997). Rather than cover much of that material, which is already in the public domain, this section of our report concentrates on the less easily available evaluations that have been carried out of the recent Workstart pilots. This evidence is of most direct relevance in informing the direction of the Government's New Deal and in itself raises many of the general points established through earlier evaluations.

Workstart employment subsidies

The last Conservative Government gave priority to improving and policing job search activity. However, it did also begin to experiment with employment subsidies and with using compulsory temporary work programmes to create an effective time limit to benefit 'dependency'.

The pilot of most direct relevance to Labour's New Deal was Workstart. This provided employment subsidies for those out of work over two years. It was piloted in four areas in 1993 where

They're very cynical

employers were offered a weekly £60 subsidy for six months, and £30 a week for the following six months. In some areas participants also received training vouchers.

Any assessment of the effects of employment subsidies has to take into account the amount of 'deadweight', where those employed would have been employed without subsidised wages; 'substitution', where subsidised employees replace non-subsidised employees; and 'displacement', where employment is drawn away from non-subsidised employers. In addition to these effects recruitment subsidies are prone to 'churning' where employers may seek a rapid staff turnover to enable them to benefit from the subsidy.

The net employment effect of a subsidy scheme may therefore be considerably less than the total number of jobs subsidised (which in turn increases the cost of each additional job created). The extent to which this is a concern to policy-makers depends on the precise net cost of subsidy schemes and the degree to which they are concerned with additionality (either for the target group or in terms of overall levels of employment) as opposed to simply helping into jobs people eligible for the subsidy even if it is at the expense of other workers or job seekers.

Two Government evaluations of Workstart confirmed that while subsidies could help some very long term unemployed people they were not a panacea for unemployment (Coopers & Lybrand, 1994; IES, 1994). Obtaining work placements involved considerable administrative effort and expense on the part of the ES and most of the jobs involved were unskilled, low paid and with very small employers. The net job creation effect of Workstart was limited and the evaluations estimated that in the pilots a new job opportunity was created in some 17% of the posts subsidised. These findings reinforced the then Government's scepticism about the value of a large scale subsidy programme which they argued would "distort the process of wage determination, and impede the efficient operation of the labour market" (ESC, 1996, iii).

Nevertheless, the previous Government did introduce another pilot phase of Workstart in 1995, covering up to 5,000 jobs, which was designed to test a range of smaller subsidies and different payment systems. After the General Election in 1997 these pilots were directly linked to the last phase of Project Work and the lessons from both programmes are now being integrated into the Labour Government's New Deal for the older long term unemployed.

The Workstart job creation results were low by international and historical standards. The results of evaluations of the impact of earlier British subsidy schemes, alongside international evidence, suggest that "the proportion of subsidised jobs which are additional typically ranges from 10 to 30 per cent" (EPI, 1997, p.70).

The impact of employment subsidies: job outcomes

Unfortunately, no control group studies of Workstart have been conducted so it is impossible to say for sure whether Workstart improved the employment prospects of participants beyond the period of the subsidy. There has been one follow up survey of Workstart participants (on the first

Welfare-to-work and the long term unemployed

Workstart pilots) which examined participants' employment status three months after the last subsidy payment to their employer. It was found that 40% were still working for the Workstart employer and a further 15% were working elsewhere (full-time, part-time or self employed) (Burtney & Littler, 1997, p. 43). The total of 55% is a fairly high job entry rate for a programme recruiting the very long-term unemployed (two years plus), and compares favourably with the rates achieved for long-term unemployed participants by work experience programmes including ILM programmes.

However, these comparisons do not provide the true picture because the selection process for participants is so different. Whereas there is little selection involved in recruitment to temporary work programmes, in order to enter an employment subsidy programme an unemployed person has to find an employer willing to employ them. Although the subsidy should make it easier to get a job, how much easier is unclear. 91% of employers who had taken part in Workstart rated "employing the best person for the job" as the most important factor when choosing a new recruit, while only 1% rated "receiving the highest subsidy" as most important (ibid, p. 33).

In other words, Workstart participants had already been through a relatively tighter selection process, and it is misleading to compare directly the outcomes of this group with a group of long-term unemployed people who have not managed to get a job and have instead entered a government programme with no direct link to an employer.

Getting a long-term unemployed person into a subsidised job obviously improves his or her job prospects over the following year, but even with a subsidy it can still be hard to get long-term unemployed people jobs. None of the Workstart pilots achieved the level of take up originally envisioned, and only between 1% and 7.5% of unemployed people eligible for the Workstart pilots entered subsidised employment over a year. It is also likely that those who did get subsidised jobs were the more 'employable' of the long-term unemployed who are likely to have had the fewest barriers to employment to begin with.

Increasing the take up of employment subsidies for the older long term unemployed, at a time when the New Deal for the younger unemployed is being marketed with a much higher profile, is going to be extremely difficult. The Workstart review found that "while an increased emphasis on marketing might be associated with higher take-up, interviews with ES staff suggested that being able to provide the right candidate for the job was as important, if not more so, than finding sufficient opportunities" (ibid, p. 50). The authors concluded that "without major changes to the scale of the programme, e.g. the level of subsidy, penetration of the eligible client group should be expected to be small (i.e. less than 5%)" (ibid, p. 50).

Employer attitudes to subsidies

All the Workstart evaluations have been based on surveys of employers rather than those recruited under the programme.

In general, employers using subsidies appear to like them (perhaps not surprisingly), though others argue that they distort the market and favour less efficient, more labour intensive working practices. The evidence on how much the subsidies change attitudes is conflicting. The Workstart survey suggests that "there was a considerable increase in employers' apparent propensity to consider recruitment of long-term unemployed people following Workstart participation" but "employers who took part had already more favourable attitudes to the long-term unemployed than employers in general" (ibid, p. 41).

There is also some evidence that subsidy regimes and payment systems can have unintended effects which can result in the targeted group being stigmatised rather than helped. When the last Australian Government rapidly expanded its Jobstart wage subsidy programme but limited eligibility to those out of work for over 18 months (as against six months) take up fell off rapidly (Finn, 1997). Evidence from the USA found this effect in a programme which made use of subsidy 'vouchers' which were issued to eligible unemployed people to present to employers as a form of self-marketing, as will be possible under the New Deal (Burtless, 1985). Indeed, one older British study also found that issuing vouchers actually reduced the chances of finding a subsidised job and Workstart employers said that "they would be suspicious of clients who presented a card if they had not heard of the programme already from another source" (Burtney & Littler, 1997, p. 27).

Work Trials

An interesting and recently used contrast with employment subsidies has been the use of Work Trials. These allow an employer to try out an unemployed person in a job for up to three weeks. In effect it reduces the recruitment 'hassle' factor and offers employers an implicit subsidy by allowing the unemployed person to receive all their state benefits plus expenses. At the end of the trial the employer guarantees to interview the participant for a regular job or give feedback through an ES adviser to unsuccessful candidates. The participant can also elect not to take the vacancy without consequences for their benefit entitlement.

Work Trials were introduced in 1989 as part of the Job Interview Guarantee Scheme and became a separate programme in 1993/94. The number of opportunities has increased each year but it is still a small programme with around 30,000 trials annually. The programme is very cheap to run, with the main costs being marketing, finding suitable employers and administration. However, the spending per trial has been cut from £92 in 1993/94 to £33 in 1996/97, and although some of this may represent more efficient administration, it is also the case that outcomes have fallen over the same period. In 1993/94, 58% of trials resulted in the participant starting work with the employer. By 1996/97 this had fallen to 50% (Hansard Written Answer, column 499, 22/12/97;

Welfare-to-work and the long term unemployed

Lourie, 1997, p. 55). A recent study of Work Trials concluded that "shortage of resource at local level appears to be an important factor in explaining variation in performance between ES offices" (Atkinson et al, 1997, p. xi)

Work Trial outcomes

As noted above over half of work trial participants get the job. After six months 51% of women and 57% of men who participated are in work (either with the original employer or with another). The key question, however, is how many of those people would have got into work anyway (deadweight). A recent control group study of Work Trials concluded that around a third of these people would have got jobs anyway, leaving a figure for job entry net of deadweight of 34% to 40% ,which is a strong result for such a cheap programme (White et al, 1997, p. 111).

There is, however, a danger that this result may be misleading in the same way as comparisons between outcomes from Workstart and those from temporary work programmes are misleading. The study is based on a matched comparison group method which means that the researchers control for all measurable differences in characteristics between those who go on a Work Trial and a control group who do not. However, the one characteristic that cannot be controlled for is the fact that the Work Trial participants have been found suitable for a vacancy in the first place and have been given a chance to prove that they can do the job.

If we examined the outcomes of unemployed people who have just secured a job interview with those who have not, we would doubtless find that more of those who had an interview were in work six months later and that getting an interview improved one's job prospects. It seems strange, however, to say that getting an interview improves ones chance of getting a job because getting an interview is 'half way' to getting a job. Since Work Trials are basically extended interviews (indeed securing a Work Trial is more likely to get one a job than securing an interview) it is not easy to compare the outcomes of those who have secured a Work Trial with those who have not.

Of course the existence of Work Trials may allow employers to try out employees they would not otherwise recruit. In this case, the question of who is selected for Work Trials becomes very important: is it those who are hardest to get into work, or do Work Trials simply 'cream off' the best recruits? The answer to this seems to be that Work Trials involve creaming. The programme is "geared towards" providing job opportunities for unemployed claimants with certain characteristics (ibid, p. 15):

- a checkable work history with references;

- qualifications or experience relevant to the types of job available through Work Trials and a desire to work in such jobs;

- possessing a telephone; and

- being highly motivated and job-ready.

They're very cynical

It is well established that all of these characteristics improve one's chance of getting work. In addition, Work Trial participants are more likely to be young, single, and have low reservation wages (the lowest wage at which they are willing to work) (White et al, 1997, p. 18-21). These characteristics are reflected in the length of time participants have been unemployed with 60% having been unemployed for under a year, and only 5% for over two years (Berry et al, p. 30).

Although Work Trials participants are more disadvantaged in terms of social class and educational qualifications this merely reflects the kind of jobs Work Trials are used for: predominantly lower grade jobs, particularly manual work in manufacturing, with fairly low average wages (£3.92 per hour in 1994/95) (ibid, p. 41). Work Trials participants have low educational qualifications but are more likely than other unemployed people to have vocational qualifications. In other words, Work Trials tend to cream off the most employable of the unemployed people competing for this particular level of jobs.

This is not to say that the existence of Work Trials has no effect on the job prospects of the eligible client group, only that they are likely to work best for people with certain characteristics.

Employer and participant opinions of Work Trials

As with Workstart, qualitative evaluation of Work Trials has concentrated on the attitudes of employers. Nevertheless, there is some evidence on claimants' attitudes, though this tends to confirm that those who it works for are the most likely to view it positively. For these people, the trial was useful "because it gave them a good idea of the work involved and helped them to decide whether or not the work suited them" (Berry et al , 1993, p. 34).

A more recent qualitative survey of very long-term unemployed people (unemployed two years plus) found that "Work Trials appeared to have generated a lot of interest". A number of people "thought that the idea of the scheme was a good one and some had tried to encourage employers to employ them on this basis" (Ritchie & Legard, 1997, p. 29).

Criticisms of Work Trials from participants focus particularly on the payment, or rather lack of it, they receive on the placement. One survey found that 59% of participants agreed with the statement that trials "are just a way of employers getting cheap labour" and the overwhelming majority felt that participants should be paid something over and above ordinary benefit payments (British Market Research Bureau, 1992). Another survey reported that "a few respondents felt that Work Trials should have some element of payment in addition to expenses, even if it was only a token amount, such as £10 per week" (Berry et al, 1993).

Employer surveys show that Work Trials were regarded as very useful by those who used them, but this was mainly a certain kind of employer: small, with "relatively unsophisticated recruitment/ selection procedures" and a "preference for selection by trial period, and distaste for paperwork and hassle" (Atkinson et al, 1997, p. ix). Trials were more likely to be used by employers with "a

Welfare-to-work and the long term unemployed

positive attitude towards the long-term unemployed or a commitment to supporting the unemployed".

It was found that the advantages of Work Trials for employers are that they are a relatively hassle free way of improving their selection process, "widening the pool of potential applicants" or reducing the costs of early leavers.

The study also found that the quality of the ES staff who act as Work Trials co-ordinators is vital to the success of the programme:

It is mainly by virtue of their high quality that employers are persuaded in, and their concerns about bureaucratic procedures set aside. Less successful offices tended to have less experienced or under-resourced co-ordinators (Atkinson et al, 1997, p. xi).

The authors recommend the promotion of "greater effectiveness in local administration of the programme" through better financing and staff training.

A lthough the success of labour market programmes is very much dependent on the overall state of the labour market there is now a considerable body of evidence to show that the way in which programmes are implemented can be crucial in max imising their impact (EC, 1992; Robinson, 1995; Nicaise et al, 1995; USA, 1995). In this respect the Employment Service will continue to play a key role. This pivotal role has already been confirmed by the Government which has made it the lead agency for delivering the New Deal. However, the Government also understood that the ES had a credibility problem with the unemployed and with employers, and with other local agencies, and from the outset it has encouraged it to develop a new approach to the unemployed. The ES has itself consulted widely about its 'values' and its performance targets and it is now trying to develop its services in new ways and work more effectively with local partnerships.

In this concluding section we draw out several key issues from the evaluation literature and consider the way in which unemployed people are selected for and recruited to programmes. In particular, we look at the role that the Employment Service and its staff can play in improving the effectiveness of programmes.

Performance targets

Over the past ten years the ES has become increasingly driven by performance targets agreed with Government. These targets are translated into regional and local expectations and in local offices have come to dominate the work of staff. Targets are also translated into contractual requirements and have also had a signigicant impact on the providers of ES programmes.

Although few would raise doubts about targets which set the timing and accuracy of benefit payments, the more difficult issues arise around targets set for job entry, referrals to programmes and, until recently, referrals to adjudication for unemployed people who did not meet the labour market conditions, such as availability for work.

The evaluation evidence we reviewed showed that there are two main ways in which the target culture of the ES has undermined the effectiveness of programmes. Firstly, targets for the number of people being referred to programmes distorts ES priorities and prevents them from delivering a fully client-centred service. A review of ES staff attitudes found that the "need to achieve start targets inevitably conflicts with trying to meet individual client needs in the most appropriate way", and uncovered a "strong feeling that [the ES] ought to be trying to develop provision which is tuned to client need rather than trying to push people into ... programmes" (Beattie, 1994, p.9). The combination of these targets and a benefits system that puts pressure on unemployed people to take up places to retain their payments means that too many people end up in programmes which are unsuitable for their needs.

Secondly, targets for the numbers of people leaving programmes for a job or a place on other training or work experience courses has led to 'creaming'. Participants are selected for programmes such as Training for Work partly on the basis of how likely they are to get a job so that the programme can meet placing targets. While job entry rates are not irrelevant to programme effectiveness they mean very little on their own, and many programmes would add far more value if they helped those with the most severe labour market disadvantages.

There is also justifiable concern that setting crude job entry rate targets has encouraged bad practice. At its most extreme it has both corrupted the collection of ES information on job placings ("Fake job figures scandal exposed", Guardian, 16/4/97) and has also created a particular form of target related fraud, with some providers fabricating evidence of job entry and qualification success.

The development of more accurate measures of performance is a complex and demanding management task, but it is crucial that in future providers and ES staff should have more input into developing those measures. If both groups are to improve the service they deliver they need to have more confidence that the performance targets they work to are useful and relevant. As Osborne and Gaebler put it, in 'Reinventing Government', "saddling people with inappropriate measures in whose development they have had no input is a sure way to create resistance, destroy morale and encourage cheating" (1993, p.358).

Developing a client-centred advice and information servicea

Unemployed people express a clear need for the provision of impartial advice and information about jobs, training and other opportunities. For example, a qualitative survey of claimant attitudes to the ES found "much criticism of ... inadequate information on training and other options open to claimants and job seekers. [Jobcentre] staff were generally believed the most helpful source of information, but they were often thought under-informed".

ES staff have also pointed to the need to rationalise programmes into "a more coherent package". The research found that there was "a general feeling that programmes and services had been developed piecemeal, to meet a particular set of economic conditions, or to satisfy political imperatives and that they do not reflect a coherent and long-term approach to helping the unemployed". In particular, staff felt that the role of the ES as a 'broker' of services and jobs to the unemployed has been "eroded by political and financial imperatives, which have little to do with getting people into jobs" (1994, p.9).

They're very cynical

To add to the complexity of choices and provision there are also employment and training options and support available outside of ES provision, including Further Education provision, Local Authority activities, TEC or LEC local initiatives and voluntary sector ESF projects.

There is a strong desire from both ES staff and unemployed claimants for a client-centred advice service with access to this broad range of provision. Unfortunately, unemployed people often find this array of support bewildering and too few ES staff know about external provision let alone having regular direct contact with their own providers.

Problems have frequently emerged around referral processes and the ability of ES staff to match unemployed people with suitable providers. For example, evaluation evidence found that many providers of Workwise, Jobplan and Project Work complained of not being kept in touch with who was to be referred to them next. Project Work providers also had "a perception that ES staff were essentially target driven which meant that the motivation to carry out a full audit of their clients' needs and aspirations would not always be there." (Ritchie & Legard, p. 78). A survey of the views of ES staff confirmed "that staff referring clients to externally contracted provision had very little direct knowledge at 'ground level' of what they were sending clients to" (Beattie, 1994, p. 6).

The New Deal for 18 to 24 year olds has started to point reform in the right direction, with its emphasis on a sequence of 'gateway' advice and counselling; followed by training, education and employment related activity; ending with a commitment to 'follow-through' support for those who need it. This approach has been underpinned by the creation of new local partnerships, individualised personal adviser support, and the development of local plans which included a mapping exercise of provision in their areas. It appears that this "partnership" approach will be gradually extended to other long term unemployed age groups with the Government indicating that there will be an increase in "local flexibility and accountability" (DfEE, 1998, p. 102). However, there will be formidable problems to overcome in translating the rhetoric of partnership into effective action and it is still not clear how these local partnerships will emerge, what their terms of reference will be, nor who they will be accountable too.

Eligibility rules, early intervention and individual entitlement

The existing system by which people become eligible for different programmes at different durations of unemployment is in need of reform. Firstly, it is far to complicated and is not understood well by claimants or staff. A report into cases dealt with by Citizens Advice Bureaux found that rationing procedures were sometimes "extremely frustrating" for claimants who were told that they had to wait several months for access to a programme or who didn't quite fit the rigid eligibility rules, for example for the Travel to Interview Scheme. The provision of information to clients about eligibility criteria was often inadequate which created a barrier to unemployed people getting the help they needed (NACAB, 1994, p. 7-9). ES staff agree that unemployed people have difficulty understanding "what is available" and often "perceive the eligibility conditions [attached] to programmes as somewhat unfair and arbitrary" (Beattie, 1994, p. 7). They also want more flexible eligibility conditions and discretion to provide access to options which are suitable for the individual (ibid, p. 10).

Most programmes currently have exemptions to the unemployment qualifying period for certain groups with particular labour market disadvantages such as ex-offenders, people with disabilities, people with literacy and numeracy difficulties, women returners, and those at risk from large scale redundancies. The list now seems arbitrary, especially as with the New Deal, when it is combined with ES adviser discretion to allow early entry to others, such as the homeless. In practice, the exemptions can also be undermined by the stress placed on securing outcome targets.

Eligibility based on duration of unemployment is also particularly unfair to those who move in and out of low paid short-term and seasonal jobs, an experience increasingly common for those leaving the unemployment register. Many of the individuals concerned are already disadvantaged in labour market terms yet if they take up these job opportunities they find it even harder to meet relevant eligibility conditions. In part, this could be remedied by using criteria based on the number of months spent in unemployment in the previous two years.

It is clear that in normal labour market conditions most people who become unemployed are able to find jobs or other options quickly (half of those claiming JSA leave unemployment within 13 weeks, and two-thirds within six months). However, while duration related eligibility rules are a useful tool for ensuring that programmes are more cost-effective it may be time for the ES to develop more sophisticated screening tools which could enable it to identify and assist those at risk of long term unemployment at an earlier stage. Early assistance could be both more effective, in building on recent work experience, and cheaper.

Although the results of an earlier 1994 ES pilot (1996) were disappointing, there has been an accumulation of evidence from the USA, Australia and Canada, where different combinations of administratively simple prescriptive models and front line discretion have produced far more positive results (Eberts and O'Leary, 1997). Indeed, a recent literature review from the Institute for Employment Research concluded that in principle "prediction of people at risk of long term unemployment is possible". The "strong statistical associations between individual characteristics, indicators of labour market demand and the incidence of prolonged unemployment are such that quite a high level of predictive power can be expected from suitable specified models" (Hasluck et al, 1997, pvi).

In the longer term it could be possible to build on the experiences of the Government's new Employment Zones to create an individual entitlement approach based on personal job accounts. If funds could be more generally allocated to areas instead of being channelled through discrete programmes, each with their own categorical and sometimes conflicting objectives and eligibility rules, greater flexibility could be created. It could then be possible that after assessing individual barriers to employment personal advisers could access a pool of funds, allocated according to the barriers faced, with which they could purchase appropriate assistance (Finn, 1997).

Benefit sanctions and programme attendance

Benefits for unemployed people in the UK have always been conditional. Availability for work and job seeking tests have been applied in various ways, and in the 1970s and 1980s participation in long duration training and wage related employment programmes, such as the Community Programme or TOPS (Training Opportunities Programme), were treated in the same way as if individual's had taken up or were offered jobs. The introduction of compulsory Restart courses in 1990, underpinned by the creation of the stricter benefit regime, led to an increase in the extent of activities that unemployed people could be compelled to participate in, culminating with the introduction of the JSA related 'Jobseekers Direction' which gives ES staff wide powers which can be used to require unemployed people to attend what are formally described as 'voluntary' programmes. The result, as our research shows, is that many of the long term unemployed are deeply sceptical about the aims and purpose of the ES.

The sanctions for failing to attend programmes have also escalated. Before JSA, the sanction for failure to attend a compulsory programme was a 40% deduction (or 20% in cases of hardship) to a claimant's weekly Income Support personal allowance for the duration of the course (one week for most courses). Under JSA regulations, the penalty involves a complete withdrawal of the entire personal allowance for two weeks for a 'first offence' followed by a four-week cut for any similar offence occurring within the next twelve months. Hardship payments are only available in limited circumstances and are not available at all to single and childless claimants for the first two weeks of the sanction. This sanction can also be imposed for failure to attend a 'voluntary' programme if a Jobseeker's Direction has been issued specifying that a claimant should attend.

Unemployed people and front line staff have mixed attitudes about compulsion. Many agree with the principle and accept it as a safeguard against abuse, yet suggest in practice it is applied inappropriately and sometimes unfairly. For example, a recent DfEE survey of people who have had their benefit cut through a sanction found that rather than these people being scroungers caught out by the system, respondents "nearly universally believed that they personally had been wrongly treated". It was the interpretation of and application of the rules in individual circumstances rather than the principle behind the rules to which respondents objected. It was also found that people with caring responsibilities, health problems or whose first language is not English were hit particularly hard by the sanctions regime (Vincent & Dobson, 1997).

Evidence from our focus groups and from studies of existing compulsory programmes illustrates a high level of dissatisfaction about being forced to work for benefit. A study of Project Work found:

> widespread opposition to the idea that people should be 'made' to work in order to continue receiving their benefits. ... Some people felt it treated long

Welfare-to-work and the long term unemployed

term unemployed people in a deprecatory or degrading way... Others thought it showed a lack of understanding or sensitivity about the needs and circumstances of people who face long term unemployment and presupposed they were 'lazy' or 'work shy' (Ritchie & Legard, 1997, p. 20).

What unemployed people resent most is compulsion without a genuine range of choice. Project Work was objected to most vehemently by those who were given little or no choice of work experience placement. It is not the compulsory nature of Restart interviews which is resented so much as the fact that unemployed people (and ES staff) feel that clients' own needs and long-term goals are ignored in favour of targets aimed at achieving short-term outcomes. Unemployed people undertaking activities such as part-time study and voluntary work which they feel will improve their long-term job prospects are perversley penalised when ES advisers require them to attend government programmes instead.

There is also evidence that providers dislike having to deal with reluctant participants who can be hard to control and disruptive to those participants who want to be there. In the Project Work pilots, for example, some voluntary organisations were reluctant to take on compulsory partici-pants because they "were concerned that it might displace their more committed volunteers" (Ritchie & Legard, 1997, p. 77).

The new Government has kept in place much of the legal framework of compulsion that it inher-ited. Indeed it has made sanctions tougher for those able bodied unemployed young people who refuse to participate in the New Deal. However, it does seem to be trying to create a different overall approach. Within the New Deal compulsion should be the last stage of a process involving individual guidance and real choice between a range of options.

For the older unemployed the aim appears to be that the requirement to attend courses should be applied more flexibly, especially in those areas which are developing programme centres. At the same time the formal targets of the ES have been amended to focus on labour market assistance rather than benefit policing measures. In practice, it will be the way these rules are applied by staff on the ground which will determine how much compulsion will emerge in the new system.

Most of the unemployed, those who work with them, and the general public, agree that individu-al's have a responsibility to engage in active job search. However, compulsory attendance on job search schemes has been a blunt weapon with which to improve their motivation and skills. The evidence from our focus groups and from ES evaluations shows that the existing culture of com-pulsion has undermined claimant confidence in the advice of the ES; results in people taking up places on often inappropriate schemes simply to protect their benefit; and it has reinforced wide-spread scepticism about the value of the courses and programmes on offer. The task now is to tackle this 'cynical' legacy by reinventing and reinvigorating the Employment Service and by creat-ing a new generation of credible and effective labour market programmes.

his research project set out to provide an independent evaluation of current UK wel fare-to-work provision for the long-term unemployed. A key aim in achieving this objective was to obtain the views and experiences of those who translate policies into action as well as those who are affected by that action. Moreover, we were concerned to obtain evidence from people that was uncontaminated by deference to authority or fear of recrimination.

The rationale for this research project and the particular way in which it was conducted reflected concerns both about the actual impact of Government policy but also about serious inadequacies in previous research in this area. In particular, much of the debate regarding welfare-to-work barriers has been abstract and too far removed from the practical realities and lived experiences of unemployed people. Equally, much research into the behaviour of unemployed people, for example in terms of their reactions to new policy initiatives, assumes that policies are implemented in a one dimensional, uniform and consistent way. Our aim was to get a better grasp of the way that unemployed people and front line staff actively negotiated about benefit rules, regulations and programme opportunities.

Indeed, to ensure that unemployed people, and those who worked with them, were able to express their views we decided to approach them independently of any formal agencies, except where access was dependent on official permission. In a day-to-day context that is often characterised by the threat of benefit penalties, or by contractual inhibitions, we felt it was vital that individual claimants and front line staff felt assured that there could be no repercussions because of what they told us.

Methodology

The enquiry was restricted to a sample based on geographical and economic criteria and conducted in four different 'case study' locations. The four areas all suffered from high unemployment and whilst registered unemployment was falling in these areas the reductions were small compared to the national average. Each area had also experienced a variety of employment and regeneration initiatives.

We aimed to talk to a total of one hundred unemployed people who had been out of work for over a year and we also wanted to talk to a range of key workers and professionals in front line agencies who worked with the long-tern unemployed in a variety of contexts and capacities. The aim was to interview a minimum of fifteen frontline people in each area totalling approximately sixty in all. Spread and depth of experience was considered more important than the classic 'representative sample' for both target groups.

Although linked by a common theme the questions we raised with each group reflected significant differences. With the long-term unemployed we wanted to find out:

- what had been their experience of looking for work and claiming benefits;

- what did they know and think about employment programmes and the active benefit system;

- how did they regard compulsory programmes and what initiatives did they think would help them get back into work; and

- what were they actually doing in terms of negotiating the benefits system and taking advantage of the opportunities available to them.

With the key workers in front-line agencies we wanted to discover:

- what they saw as the main barriers faced by the long term unemployed;

- how had their work has been affected by the stricter benefit regime and compulsory programmes;

- how did they make sense of the actual process of turning new policies and benefit flexibilities into day to day realities; and

- in what ways did they think programmes could be made more relevant and/or effective.

In seeking answers to these 'how and why' type questions, in preference to 'what and when' type information, a qualitative case study approach was thought the most appropriate (Yin, 1989). The particular research methods chosen for each group were selected on the basis of best practice achievable with the available resources.

We adopted focus groups with the long-term unemployed, not just because they are in fashion with Government, but because the evidence shows that the group interview is particularly useful for understanding the reaction and perception of an affected population to a policy change (Frey & Fontana, 1993). Focus groups are often adopted when there is a power differential between participants and decision-makers. The interaction within the group, coupled with the security of being among peers is likely to encourage participants to share views that they might otherwise be reluctant to divulge (Morgan & Krueger, 1993). Focus groups are also an effective way to investigate complex behaviour and motivations:

They're very cynical

By comparing the different points of view that participants exchange during the interactions in focus groups, researchers can examine motivation with a degree of complexity that is typically not available with other methods (ibid, p. 16).

Focus groups generate their own structure and meaning and can provide access to the group's level of meaning (Denzin, 1989). More significantly, focus groups are particularly useful when a research method is required that is friendly, respectful and non-condescending. This is an important consideration when researching a group such as the long term unemployed who are all too often treated with low esteem.

Our focus group participants were selected and recruited via an initial screening questionnaire administered just outside Employment Service Jobcentres (ESJs). The permission of ESJ managers to do this work was considered but then rejected in case it was not granted. Moreover, early experience demonstrated that recruitment would have been almost impossible if potential participants felt that there was any connection between this research and the ES. Anonymity was guaranteed for claimants.

The ideal size of a focus group is thought to be somewhere between six and ten participants. Standard practice is to over-recruit by 20% in case of non-attendance (Morgan, 1993). It was initially envisaged that three focus groups would be held in each area to which between eight and ten participants would be invited. Two of the groups in each area would be exclusively male and the third group exclusively female. This strategy had several distinct advantages: it simplified the screening procedure and quota sampling; it reflected the gender balance criteria; and it helped to overcome the problems associated with male domination of group discussions. In practice, smaller groups of between five and six participants proved to be more productive. The focus groups were scheduled to last for two hours but most lasted longer at the discretion of the participants.

Interviews with key workers in front line agencies

Because we needed to seek information from as wide a range of key workers as possible we decided to use face to face in-depth interviews. Semi-structured interviews were deemed more suitable than pre-determined questionnaires in this particular study, not least because of the open-ended nature of the enquiry (Robson, 1993).

Semi-structured face-to-face interviews were conducted with a total of 48 people. They were employed in a variety of capacities in a range of key organisations and were based in forty different locations in the four areas. The organisations included the Employment Service, contracted programme providers, voluntary and statutory training providers, FE colleges, advice agencies and support groups. Most of the interviews were with frontline workers although company directors and managers were also interviewed. These interviews lasted between one and two hours each and were tape-recorded. Most of the interviews were conducted in the workplace setting of the

Welfare-to-work and the long term unemployed

interviewee although some were conducted in private locations where it was inconvenient to use the workplace.

Most of the organisations that were contacted were extremely helpful and cooperative although there were some notable exceptions. For example some ESJ managers were cooperative others were not. Equally some contracted providers were similarly reluctant to allow their staff to talk to us. As mentioned earlier, we were concerned to obtain evidence from providers that was uncontaminated by deference to authority or sponsoring organisations. In cases where official permission to interview staff of organisations was denied, front line workers were approached directly and informally. Although many key workers were reluctant to talk to us because of fear of recriminations, most were willing to be interviewed with the following provisos:

- in the majority of cases individuals working within organisations stated that they would only talk to us on the understanding that neither they nor the organisation would be identified; and

- some heads of organisations would not talk to us if there were any possibility of the sponsoring agency (e.g. TECs and the ES) being able to identify them.

Sampling and profiles

The sample of one hundred long-term unemployed people was not intended to be representative though we did use quotas in order to get as wide a variety of participants as possible differentiated by age, race, gender and family responsibilities. Age categories and quotas reflect those used in the claimant count as given in Labour Market Trends. The ethnic composition of the focus groups reflected as far as possible the ethnic mix of the local community. The gender balance reflected the broad ratio of male/female registered unemployed throughout the country (one third female/two thirds male). In terms of family responsibilities, participants reflected a range of circumstances including marital status and childcare responsibilities.

Three focus groups were conducted in each of the four locations and ten people were invited to each group (over recruiting by 20%). A total of seventy eight long term unemployed people actually participated in the focus groups.

The shortfall was due to non-attendance, which could not be anticipated accurately and despite deliberately over-recruiting by the recommended 20%. There was a surprising amount of difficulty recruiting focus group participants due largely to suspicion and mistrust on the part of jobseekers. There was also a high degree of scepticism and cynicism on the part of those who attended the focus groups as to the value of the research. These factors may go some way to explaining the level of non-attendance. There was also difficulty locating and recruiting sufficient female focus group participants to fulfil the predicted 2:1 male/female ratio.

They're very cynical

Overall:

- twenty six participants (33.3%) had been unemployed for over five years and nine of these (11.5% of sample) had child care/ family responsibilities;

- five participants (6.9%) had been unemployed for ten or more years;

- the longest duration was fifteen years (black male, aged 31, who had never worked);

- 42.3 % of the sample had child care/family responsibilities; and

- 19.2% of the sample were from Black/Asian ethnic minorities.

This information is for illustrative purposes only and has no direct statistical value. Those unemployed people we approached were not a representative sample of all unemployed people but represented a random sample of people exiting Jobcentres.

Table 4: Profile of focus group participants

	Aged 25-29	30-39	40-49	50-59	Child care duties	Black/ Asian ethnic minority
Men	9	17	19	12	22	11
Women	8	9	2	2	11	4
%	22%	33%	27%	18%	n/a	n/a
Unemployed 1-2 years	5	5	4	1	8	4
2-3 years	3	6	8	0	7	4
3-4 years	5	4	2	2	5	4
4-5 years	0	2	2	3	4	1
Over 5 years	4	9	5	8	9	2

The sample of fifteen key workers in each area was gathered on the following basis:

- four providers delivering ES programmes such as Restart, Jobplan and Jobclub;
- four ES frontline staff including Client Advisers involved in intensive counselling programmes;
- four from training and education providers delivering ESF, TfW and FE courses for unemployed people;
- three advice workers, including adult guidance workers from colleges, staff in support groups and Welfare Rights Officers.

In addition, we also spoke to a number of former employees of the ES and private companies delivering ES programmes.

Welfare-to-work and the long term unemployed

Ways of estimating outcomes net of deadweight

Randomised trials

The ideal control group study method is a randomised trial in which people are randomly assigned to either the programme group (who have access to the programme) or the control group (who do not). So long as a large enough sample is used for the study then the random assignment to the groups will ensure that there are no significant differences between the circumstances of the two groups other than that one has access to the programme while the other does not.

The ideal control group study method is a randomised trial in which people are randomly assigned to either the programme group (who have access to the programme) or the control group (who do not). So long as a large enough sample is used for the study then the random assignment to the groups will ensure that there are no significant differences between the circumstances of the two groups other than that one has access to the programme while the other does not.ideal control group study method is a randomised trial in which people are randomly assigned to either the programme group (who have access to the programme) or the control group (who do not). So long as a large enough sample is used for the study then the random assignment to the groups will ensure that there are no significant differences between the circumstances of the two groups other than that one has access to the programme while the other does not.control group study method is a randomised trial in which people are randomly assigned to either the programme group (who have access to the programme) or the control group (who do not). So long as a large enough sample is used for the study then the random assignment to the groups will ensure that there are no significant differences between the circumstances of the two groups other than that one has access to the programme while the other does not.

While this kind of study has been conducted, notably in evaluations of compulsory programmes such as Restart interviews and Jobplan Workshops, it has been found difficult to apply to other programmes, principally because it is difficult to justify refusing access to a programme to one group while allowing others who attend the same Jobcentre and are in the same circumstances to participate.

While this kind of study has been conducted, notably in evaluations of compulsory programmes such as Restart interviews and Jobplan Workshops, it has been found difficult to apply to other programmes, principally because it is difficult to justify refusing access to a programme to one group while allowing others who attend the same Jobcentre and are in the same circumstances to participate.this kind of study has been conducted, notably in evaluations of compulsory programmes such as Restart interviews and Jobplan Workshops, it has been found difficult to apply to other programmes, principally because it is difficult to justify refusing access to a programme to one group while allowing others who attend the same Jobcentre and are in the same circumstances to participate.this kind of study has been conducted, notably in evaluations of compulsory programmes such as Restart interviews and Jobplan Workshops, it has been found difficult to apply to other programmes, principally because it is difficult to justify refusing access to a programme to one group while allowing others who attend the same Jobcentre and are in the same circumstances to participate.

Pilot programmes: tracking studies and register effects

Some programmes are introduced in a number of pilot regions first which allows evaluation by undertaking a tracking study and/or an analysis of register off-flows. These techniques have been central to the evaluation of Workwise courses and 1-2-1 supportive caseloading.

Pilot programmes: tracking studies and register effectsSome programmes are introduced in a number of pilot regions first which allows evaluation by undertaking a tracking study and/or an analysis of register off-flows. These techniques have been central to the evaluation of Workwise courses and 1-2-1 supportive caseloading.Pilot programmes: tracking studies and register effectsSome programmes are introduced in a number of pilot regions first which allows evaluation by undertaking a tracking study and/or an analysis of register off-flows. These techniques have been central to the evaluation of Workwise courses and 1-2-1 supportive caseloading.Pilot programmes: tracking studies and register effectsSome programmes are introduced in a number of pilot regions first which allows evaluation by undertaking a tracking study and/or an analysis of register off-flows. These techniques have been central to the evaluation of Workwise courses and 1-2-1 supportive caseloading.

A tracking study is used to compare the outcomes of those referred to the new programme with a control group of participants in similar circumstances in areas not operating the programme. For example, in 1994 Workwise courses were introduced on a pilot basis in a number of ES offices. 18 to 24 year olds signing on in the pilot offices that refused all other offers at their twelve month Restart interview were referred to Workwise. The control group comprised 18 to 24 year olds who refused all offers of help at the twelve month Restart interview and signed on outside the pilot offices. The destinations of the two groups were then compared.A tracking study is used to compare the outcomes of those referred to the new programme with a control group of participants in similar circumstances in areas not operating the programme. For example, in 1994 Workwise courses were introduced on a pilot basis in a number of ES offices. 18 to 24 year olds signing on in the pilot offices that refused all other offers at their twelve month Restart interview were referred to Workwise. The control group comprised 18-24 year olds who refused all offers of help at the twelve month Restart interview and signed on outside the pilot offices. The destinations of the two groups were then compared. tracking study is used to compare the outcomes of those referred to the new programme with a control group of participants in similar circumstances in areas not operating the programme. For example, in 1994 Workwise courses were introduced on a pilot basis in a number of ES offices. 18 to 24 year olds signing on in the pilot offices that refused all other offers at their twelve month Restart interview were referred to Workwise. The control group comprised 18-24 year olds who refused all offers of help at the twelve month Restart interview and signed on outside the pilot offices. The destinations of the two groups were then compared. tracking study is used to compare the outcomes of those referred to the new programme with a control group of participants in similar circumstances in areas not operating the programme. For example, in 1994 Workwise courses were introduced on a pilot basis in a number of ES offices. 18 to 24 year olds signing on in the pilot offices that refused all other offers at their twelve month Restart interview were referred to Workwise. The control group comprised 18-24 year olds who refused all offers of help at the twelve month Restart interview and signed on outside the pilot offices. The destinations of the two groups were then compared.

This is not a randomised trial because allocation to the programme group or control group is on the basis of where one lives rather than being random. A tracking study is a fairly good alternative to a randomised trial, but is less reliable, principally because there could be significant differences between the pilot areas and the control areas which cannot be captured by an analysis of the characteristics of the two groups, for example local labour market conditions could differ significantly.

Because of these problems, a comparison of pilot and control areas is often supplemented by an analysis of register off-flows. This involves using statistics from government databases on unemployed benefit claimants to examine any changes in the numbers of people from specific groups (e.g. 18 to 24 year olds) leaving the unemployment register in particular areas. If significant changes are observed in pilot areas at the same time as a new programme is introduced then it may be that those changes can be attributed to the programme.

The biggest problem with this method is that it is extremely difficult to separate out the effect of other factors which may be causing any changes such as local labour market conditions or other changes to the operation of the benefit system. A further problem is that it is not possible to track the actual destinations of people leaving the register

Matched comparison method

The evaluation methods considered above are generally unsuitable for voluntary programmes because people cannot be allocated to a group who will take part in the programme. The alternative which has been used is the matched comparison method, which involves using as the programme group a number of people who chose to attend the programme, then constructing a control group of people who did not attend the programme but whose characteristics match those of the programme group. For example, the control group should contain the same proportion of men and women as the programme group, the same proportion of long term unem-

They're very cynical

ployed, the same spread of ages, skills and work experience, etc. The idea is to match the two groups on as many attributes known to affect employment prospects as possible.

Inevitably it is not possible to match the two groups exactly, so statistical techniques are then used to account for any difference in outcomes between the groups which result from differences between the characteristics of the groups rather than from participation on the programme.

With an appropriate sample size and detailed information on the characteristics of everyone included in the study the matched comparison method can give a fair indication of the difference a programme makes to individuals' outcomes. Nevertheless the matched comparison method is far from perfect. The main unresolved problem is that the people who choose to go on the programme may be exactly those people who are most ready to get a job.

Atkinson J and Jillage J (1993) *The costs of getting a job (for the Employment Service)*, Institute of Manpower Studies.

Atkinson J and Meager N (1994) *Evaluation of Workstart Pilots*, Institute for Employment Studies.

Atkinson J, Giles L, Meager N (1996) *Temployers, Recruitment and the Unemployed*, Institute for Employment Studies.

Atkinson J, Kodz J, Tackey N, Barber L, O'Regan S (1997) *Work Trials employer study*, Institute for Employment Studies.

Balls E and Gregg P (1993) *Work and welfare: tackling the jobs deficit*, Institute for Public Policy Research.

Beattie C (1994) *Strategic review of jobseeker services: report on the view of staff*, Research and Evaluation Report no. 102, Employment Service.

Berry C, Harrison J and Radley C (1993) *Evaluation of the Work Trial Pilots:main report*, Research and Evaluation Report no. 85, Employment Service.

Birtwhistle A, Barnes D and Looby C (1994) *Evaluation of Supportive Caseloading (1-2-1) in North Norfolk: tracking study*, Research and Evaluation Report no. 95, Employment Service.

Birtwhistle A and Looby C (1994) *Jobplan evaluation: analysis of register off flows*, Research and Evaluation Report no. 99, Employment Service.

Blagg N, Ballinger M and Lewis R (1994) *Quality in Jobplan Workshops: final report (for the Employment Service)*, Nigel Blagg Associates.

Bottomly D, McKay S and Walker R (1997) *Unemployment and Jobseeking*, DSS Research Report no. 62, Stationery Office.

British Market Research Bureau (1992) *Summary of a report of JIG participants* (for the Employment Service).

Bryson C (1995) *Travel to Interview Scheme (for the Employment Service)*, Public Attitude Surveys.

Bryson C (1995a) *Community Action Participants Survey (for the Employment Service)*, Public Attitude Surveys.

Burtless G (1985) '*Are Targeted Wage Subsidies Harmful? Evidence from a Wage Voucher Experiment*', Industrial and Labor Relations Review, issue 39, USA.

Burtney E and Littler C (1997) *Workstart Review*, Research and Evaluation Report no. 114, Employment Service.

Cambridge Policy Consultants (1996) *Glasgow Works evaluation: final report*, Glasgow Development Agency.

Cragg Ross and Dawson (1993) *1993 Employment Service Customer Satisfaction Survey: qualitative research* (for the Employment Service).

CLES (1996) *Regeneration Through Work*, Centre for Local Economic Strategies, Manchester.

They're very cynical

CRG (1994) *A Qualitative Evaluation of the North Norfolk Pilots* (for the Employment Service)

Daniel W W (1990) *The Unemployed Flow*, Policy Studies Institute.

Deacon A (1997) *'Benefit sanctions for the jobless: 'tough love' or rough treatment'*, Economic Report vol. 11, no. 7, Employment Policy Institute.

Department of Employment (1990) *Motivation, Unemployment and Employment Department Programmes,* DE Research Paper 80.

Department for Education and Employment (1997) *Design of the New Deal for 18-24 year olds.*

Donnelly, C (1997) *Chance of a Lifetime,* Unemployment Unit.

Donnelly, C (1997a) *'Adult guidance for the unemployed and the new Labour Government',* Working Brief issue 84, p.24-26, Unemployment Unit.

Dutton P and LcLaughlin D (1996) *A guide to the calculation of net excheequer costs per person off the count,* Research and Evaluation Report no. 108, Employment Service.

Duxbury L and Ward H (1993) *Evaluation of Job Search Seminars,* Research and Evaluation Report no. 82, Employment Service.

DVL Smith Ltd (1994) *Jobplan and 12 Month Flow Evaluation*: research report (for the Employment Service).

EC (1992) ERGO Programme Phase One, Final Report, *Directorate-General for Employment, Industrial Relations and Social Affairs,* Commission of the European Communities, 1992.

Employment Service (1994) *Workwise Leaders Manual.*

Employment Service (1997) *New Deal Operational Vision.*

ESC (1996) *Government Response to the Second Report from the Employment Committee, Session 1995-96:* The Right to Work/Workfare, Annex, HMSO.

ESC (1997) *The New Deal, House of Commons Education and Employment Committee, Second Report,* Vol II, HC 263-II, HMSO.

Finn D (1986) *'Half Measures',* Unemployment Bulletin, issue 19, p. 1-5.

Finn D (1988) *'The CP Experience',* Unemployment Bulletin issue 26, p. 17-21.

Finn D (1993) *'The Restart effect: does Restart reduce unemployment',* Working Brief issue 43, p.9-11, Unemployment Unit.

Finn D (1995) *'Travel to Interview Scheme: changes in the pipeline',* Working Brief issue 64, p.5-7, Unemployment Unit.

Finn D (1997) *Working Nation: welfare reform and the Australian Job Compact for the long-term unemployed,* Unemployment Unit.

Frey J H and Fontana A (1993) *The Group Interview in Social Research,* ch.2 in: Morgan D L, [ed] (1993) op cit.

Gardiner K (1997) *Bridges from benefit to work: a review,* Joseph Rowntree Foundation.

Heather P and Kay J (1995) *Job Review Workshop evaluation,* Research and Evaluation Report no. 106, Employment Service.

H.M. Treasury (1997) *The modernisation of Britain's tax and benefit system (no. 1):* employment opportunity in a changing labour market.

Kay J (1994) *Jobplan evaluation: tracking study,* Research and Evaluation Report no. 98, Employment Service.

Welfare-to-work and the long term unemployed

Kay J, Gibbins C and Birtwhistle A (1995) *Evaluation of Workwise/Worklink pilots for 18-24 year-olds: tracking study and analysis of register off-flows*, Research and Evaluation Report no. 104, Employment Service.

Kay J, Gibbins C and Birtwhistle A (1995a) *Evaluation of 1-2-1 supportive caseload pilots for 18-24 year-olds: tracking study and analysis of register off-flows*, Research and Evaluation Report no. 105, Employment Service.

Kay J and Fletcher J (1996) *Evaluation of 1-2-1/ Workwise for 18-24 year-olds: tracking study*, Research and Evaluation Report no. 109, Employment Service.

Killeen J (1996) *Does guidance work? An evaluation of the intermediate outcomes of Gateways to Learning*, Research Study RS19, Department for Education and Employment.

Layard R (1995) *Preventing Long-Term Unemployment*, Employment Policy Institute.

Lourie J (1997) *Employment and training schemes for the unemployed*, Research Paper 97/ 98, House of Commons Library.

Manpower Services Commission (1984) *Community Programme postal follow-up survey*.

McGregor A, Ferguson Z, Fitzpatrick I, McConnachie M and Richmond K (1997) *Bridging the jobs gap: an evaluation of the Wise Group and the intermediate labour market*, Joseph Rowntree Foundation.

McKay S, Walker R and Youngs R (1997) *Unemployment and Jobseeking before Jobseeker's Allowance*, DSS Research Report no. 73, Stationery Office.

Morgan D L (1988) *Focus Groups As Qualitative Research*, Sage.

Morgan D L [ed] (1993) *Successful Focus Groups: Advancing the State of the Art*, Sage.

Morgan D L and Krueger R A (1993) *'When to Use Focus Groups and Why'*, ch.1 in: Morgan D L, [ed] (1993) op cit.

Murray I (1996) *'Compulsion is not working'*, Working Brief issue 71, p. 17-21, Unemployment Unit.

Murray I (1996a) *'Stricter Benefits Regime scales new heights'* Working Brief issue 77, p. 18-21, Unemployment Unit.

Murray I (1996b) *'Short-term unemployed denied help with fares to interviews'* Working Brief issue 76, p. 4-6, Unemployment Unit.

Murray I (1997) *'Modular jobsearch programmes being piloted'* Working Brief issue 87, p. 9-10, Unemployment Unit.

Murray I (1997a) *'Employment Service targets under review'* Working Brief issue 88, p. 15-18, Unemployment Unit.

Murray I (1997b) *'Modular jobsearch programmes being piloted'* Working Brief issue 87, p. 9-10, Unemployment Unit.

NACAB (1994) *In search of work: CAB evidence on employment and training programmes for unemployed people*, National Association of Citizens Advice Bureaux.

Nicaise I et al (1995), *Labour Market Programmes For The Poor in Europe: Pitfalls and Dilemmas - And How To Avoid Them*, Aldershot, Avebury.

Nimmo M (1996) *'Welfare myths challenged by Government's own research'*, Working Brief issue 80, p. 19-22, Unemployment Unit.

Nimmo M (1997) *'Housing policies have set the unemployment and poverty traps'*, Working Brief issue 86, p. 6-8, Unemployment Unit.

Nimmo M (1997a) *'Benefit traps and the potential for Intermediate Labour Markets'*, Working Brief issue 89, p. 17-19, Unemployment Unit.

Nove A and Smith N (1995) *Employment Service National Customer Satisfaction Survey 1994,* Research and Evaluation Report no. 103, Employment Service.

Osborne D, Gaebler T (1993) *Reinventing Government,* Plume Books, New York.

Payne J, Lissenburgh S, White M (1996) *Employment Training and Employment Action,* DFEE Research Report No. 74, Policy Studies Institute/Department for Education and Employment.

Public Attitude Surveys Ltd (1996) *Restart Course Postal Survey* (for the Employment Service).

Public Attitude Surveys Ltd (1997) *Community Action Follow-up* (for the Employment Service).

Quality Assurance Division (1994) *Factors maximising job outcomes in TfW,* Employment Department Quality Assurance Division.

Ritchie J and Legard R (1997) *The first Project Work pilots: a qualitative evaluation,* DFEE Research Report RR30, Department for Education and Employment.

Robinson P (1995) *'The Limits of Active Labour Market Policies',* Economic Report Vol 9, No 6, Employment Policy Institute.

Robson C (1993) *Real World Research: A Resource for Social Scientists and Practitioner-researchers,* Blackwell, Oxford.

Scott G (1995) *'Active Labour Market Policies: Let's be Careful Out There',* Social Policy Journal of New Zealand Issue 5.

Shaw A et al (1996) *Moving off Income Support: barriers and bridges,* DSS Research Report no. 53, HMSO.

Smith N and Stallwood N (1994) *Employment Service National Customer Satisfaction Survey 1993,* Research and Evaluation Report no. 93, Employment Service.

USA (1995), What's Working (and What's Not): A Summary of Research on the Economic Impacts of Employment and Training Programs, Office of the Chief Economist, US Department of Labor.

Vincent J and Dobson B (1997) *Jobseeker's Allownace Evaluation: Qualitative Research on Disallowed and Disqualified Claimants,* DFEE Research Report RR15, Department for Education and Employment.

Webster D (1997) *'Welfare to work: why the theories behind the policies don't work',* Working Brief issue 85, p. 10-11, Unemployment Unit.

White M and Lakey J (1992) *The Restart effect: does active labour market policy reduce unemployment?,* Policy Studies Institute (for the Employment Service).

White M, Lissenburgh S and Bryson A (1997) *The Impact of Public Job Placing Programmes,* Policy Studies Institute.

Wright E and Cooper G (1996) *Qualitative evaluation of 1-2-1/Workwise (for the Employment Service),* Elsa Wright Associates.

Yin R K, (1989) *Case Studies Research (2nd edn)* Sage, Newbury Park, California.